THE INTROVERT'S GUIDE TO JOB HUNTING

How To Outshine The Competition

By Tim Toterhi

The Introvert's Guide to Job Hunting
ALL RIGHTS RESERVED.
Copyright © 2015 Tim Toterhi

Cover Design by Stephannie Beman, stephanniebeman.com/design-portfolio
Cover Photography by Wavebreakmedia Ltd of Dreamstime.com
Edited by Keith Miller

Published by Plotline Leadership

Print ISBN: 978-0-9860646-8-5
ebook ISBN: 978-0-9860646-7-8

Table of Contents

The Introvert's Guide to Job Hunting

Ready, Set ... Wait, Let Me Process!

Before We Begin

Why does the world need another book on the job-search process? That's the first question I asked myself when I set out to write *The Introvert's Guide to Job Hunting*. After all, a quick scan of Amazon's listings reveals dozens of titles on the subject. And that doesn't include the variety of in-store options that are available. There's a lot of great material out there ... and a lot of misguided nonsense.

Still, there was something missing. As an introvert, I've often thought the strategies presented in most books are targeted to the estimated 66 percent of the U.S. population classified as extroverts on the Myers-Briggs Type Indicator (MBTI). Most people experience a bit of nervousness during the interview process, but for an introvert these quasi-social events can be draining.

Don't get me wrong. Introverts are not the social misfits they are sometimes portrayed to be. Many professional actors and comedians are off-the-chart introverts who develop a workaround that allows them to stand before groups large and small in the most trying of settings. As a seasoned trainer and keynote speaker, I've learned to work a room like nobody's business. And I'm sure you've also managed to rise to the occasion in your chosen profession, whether the task called for public speaking, navigating client dinners, or quickly responding to requests in a social setting.

We can do it – it's just not our first choice of activity. Left to our own devices, we'd be much happier avoiding the idle corporate chitchat and instead getting down to business. And while "letting your work do the talking" is a reasonable philosophy in a setting where you are a known commodity, it doesn't play well in the job-search process.

The Introvert's Guide to Job Hunting leverages proven research, new thought leadership, and practical experience. It is designed to leverage your strengths in preparation for the interview process while filling gaps and securing lessons from those who are naturally extroverted. This three-phase book will help you:

- assess your professional potential through a series of targeted career assessments,
- develop a "rock star" resume and cover letter that will secure you interviews, and, most important,
- learn specific techniques that will help you become a master interviewee.

The Introvert's Guide to Job Hunting is packed with over forty exercises and tools that will help you actively navigate the job-search process. As a human resources professional with over fifteen years of experience in a variety of industries, companies, and countries, I've seen the effectiveness of these tools firsthand.

In addition to the material presented, readers will gain the perspectives of expert staffing professionals who specialize in temporary or contract hires, traditional full-time corporate staff, and executive-level professionals. We'll also hear from seasoned corporate coaches and headhunters to gain their perspective on the process. Wherever you are in your career – fresh graduate or experienced professional – *The Introvert's Guide to Job Hunting* can help you take it to the next level.

But What About Extroverts?

Leverage Strengths, Reduce Liabilities

While it's true that extroverts may be comfortable with the interview process, job hunting is stressful for everyone. *The Introvert's Guide to Job Hunting* can help extroverts by offering solid reminders of how to approach the discussion portion of the process (often a clear strength). More important, it can provide a framework for doing the type of career analysis that is often overlooked.

By following the exercises outlined in this book, extroverts can become even *more* effective in the interview process. In short, although this was written with fellow introverts in mind, it is ideal for anyone seeking to change jobs, switch careers, or advance in their current organization.

Additional Support

The Introvert's Guide to Job Hunting contains everything you need to assess your professional potential and make informed choices about your career. Some readers, though, may be interested in additional personalized coaching or training. If you'd like to learn more about the services noted below, visit www.plotlineleadership.com.

- **Career Coaching:** My clients have the opportunity to complete a self-assessment that tailors the content and tools in this book to their specific needs. Concepts can be presented in discussion format over the phone or via individualized in-person coaching sessions.
- **Group Training:** The concepts presented in this book are also available in traditional instructor-led format. Customized agendas and formats are available.

Regardless of the additional support selected, my goal is to ensure each participant completes the engagement with a clear, achievable career action plan.

Phase 1 – Assessing Your Professional Potential

Purpose

The first step in any journey is preparation. Embark without a clear destination and the right tools to keep you on track and you could find yourself lost or, worse, stranded on the side of the road.

Career changes are journeys of a different sort. Whether you are seeking a job in a new company, changing departments, or switching careers entirely, it's crucial that you properly prepare for the adventure ahead. Performing a self-assessment once or twice per year will help you avoid career stalls and spinouts. In addition, the tools described in this phase will help you explore all possible routes, select the best one for you, and ensure that each step you take moves you toward your desired destination.

Description

This phase is designed to help the career-minded quickly acquire an accurate picture of their marketable skills and interests, as well as an understanding of those areas that require further development. Whether you're looking to change jobs, refocus your career, or simply add a new level of fulfillment to your current position, this phase will help you reach your goal. Specifically, Phase 1 will help you:

- List and describe your interests, skills, and values
- Describe your Personal Value Proposition (PVP)
- Monitor and gauge your relationships with colleagues and your manager
- Develop an understanding of your preferred company structure, norms, and culture
- Recognize, analyze, and select various career options
- Understand the importance of lateral moves and personal-development opportunities
- Create alliances with key people in your organization or desired occupation
- Develop a plan for career growth and continued training

Introduction

There is nothing more frustrating than succeeding in the wrong direction.

People instinctively strive for advancement. Many of us long for more responsibility, seek greater challenges, and revel in the chance to be tested on new and exciting projects. For all the talk of people's natural fear of change, many crave change and the opportunities it presents.

So why then do these change seekers so often second-guess their actions? Why is it that when these career-minded individuals switch jobs, relocate, or accept a promotion, they find themselves less happy than they were before the move was made?

Some attribute this feeling to longer hours, increased workload, or a shift in colleagues. Others call it nostalgia, pointing to the greener grass growing in the home of our yesteryear. But neither answer is sufficient. Motivated people make career moves precisely for the opportunity to go beyond that which they have outgrown. Most understand that the price of this growth is hard work.

Often people find themselves unsatisfied with their work situation because they neglected to take the first and most important step in any job change or career transition: a self-assessment. Without a detailed understanding of who you are and what you want, it is doubtful that you will ever paint a clear picture of where you wish to go.

Phase 1 of this book is a three-part self-assessment process designed to help you make sense of your career.

- **Part 1** will help you define a subjective self-view of your career interests, skills, and values. It will also help you develop a personal value proposition (PVP) that will distinguish you from the competition.
- **Part 2** will examine your current work reality in terms of five core success factors. It will also review the road you took to get there.
- Finally, **Part 3** will use this information to help you craft a workable career plan designed to improve your situation and attain a position you can truly be passionate about.

As you move through this phase, you will begin to understand yourself and your decisions like never before. This heightened self-awareness will not only help you achieve your career aspirations; it will also improve your relationships with others and your self-knowledge.

As an introvert, you likely have a leg up in this regard. The process, however, requires more than a natural inclination. It takes active involvement on your part. To get the most out of your study, take the time to fully complete the exercises in this book. Remember that to achieve success in any endeavor you must:

- Obtain an empowering **perspective** on your goals – both *where you are* in your career and *where you wish to go.*
- Have the **persistence** to see the process to completion.
- Muster the **creativity** to navigate hurdles as they appear.

I firmly believe that, whatever your current circumstance, thoughtful planning and concrete action can help you navigate your way to the next level.

Assessment Guidelines

The self-assessment cannot be successful without your full participation. To ensure the accuracy and usability of the results you must have the courage to put yourself in the HOT seat. By that, I mean you need to be willing to be Honest, Objective, and Thorough:

- **Honest**: Holding back, ignoring your true interests, or committing to something out of habit or a sense of obligation could not only render the assessment ineffective; it could put you on an improper career path.
- **Objective**: Try to put your emotions on hold and answer the questions objectively. Ask a trusted friend or colleague to validate all the opinions you note about yourself.
- **Thorough**: Complete all parts of the assessments and take additional notes when needed. The more details you discover about yourself, the more revealing the process will be.

Rules of the Road

People embark on journeys for a variety of reasons – recreation, study, or simply the thrill of viewing the unseen. Changing jobs and/or switching careers are expeditions of a different sort. Though they may not be our first travel choice, we can make the trip successful by following some fundamental rules of the road.

- **Have a clear reason for traveling** – Are you running *toward* a career opportunity or *away* from a bad job situation?

- **Select an appropriate destination** – Are you clear about what you want in the new role or company?

- **Pack what you need** – Have you developed the skills, experience, and tools needed to make the journey?

- **Leave behind that which will weigh you down** – Have you taken the time to learn from past mistakes and adjust your game plan as needed?

- **Be aware of pitfalls that will spoil the trip** – Have you researched how others succeeded or stumbled in the role you want?

- **Design a plan to ensure you get where you want to go** – Will you take the time to develop a GPS for career success?

- **Don't be ashamed to ask for directions** – Have you found a mentor or coach who can guide you on your way?

Although *The Introvert's Guide to Job Hunting* is written for individual participants to navigate on their own, you will get even more out of this book by reviewing the exercises with your career coach. If you'd like more information on career coaching or team training on this topic, visit www.plotlineleadership.com. For now, let's begin by reviewing your current situation.

Coach Exercise 1: Viewing Your Plan

Get into the habit of consulting your travel guide (career coach). Take a few minutes to bring him or her up to speed on where you are in your career and what you hope to achieve by reading this book.

Don't have a coach yet? No worries. Just take a few minutes to talk it out and then write it down. Remember, if you can't say it, you can't do it.

Reviewing Your Plan

Part 1: Your Self-View

Before jumping into a formal assessment process it is usually a good idea to take a look at the larger issues. The following exercises will serve as a foundation for the job-specific analysis ahead. It will give you the opportunity to reflect on past experiences and confirm or call into question the assumptions others may have made about you as well as those you accepted as your personal truth.

As we move through the assessment, the following formula is important to keep in mind:

Personality + Interests + Skills + Values = Your PVP

Your Personal Value Proposition (PVP) highlights what you (and you alone) can bring to the desired position. This can inform the choice of vehicle (career) to drive you to success.

Personal Branding: Defining Your PVP

We're all familiar with the phrase "selling yourself," but can we effectively put the concept into practice? Before you can think about crafting a resume or navigating an interview, you have to be acutely aware of what you have to offer a current or potential employer. This goes far beyond a listing of work experiences and educational credentials. To make the sale you have to stand out, and that involves clearly articulating your PVP.

While this process can be tough for anyone, it can be particularly trying for introverts, who may not be comfortable with the idle small talk that often precedes the elevator speech. Luckily there is a formula to follow – a method of training yourself to enable your PVP to emerge naturally.

Great marketers know that in most cases people don't buy a product or service, they buy the feeling or effect that product or service can deliver. For example, people don't set out to buy sugar water. They buy refreshment. Whether that comes in the form of a *crisp classic* or in the form of membership in a *new generation* is a distinction worth billions. It seems silly in the context of a beverage, but without branding, you're representing the generic offering: the replaceable, commoditized, third-tier cola that is lucky to pick up the scraps of the market left by the major players.

Now apply this concept to what you do. Whether you're a salesperson or a scientist, a project manager or a publicist, there are literally thousands – and in some cases millions – of people who do exactly what you do for a living. So how can you avoid becoming the interchangeable part of the profession? How can you stand out?

Part of the answer has to do with your education, skills, and the experiences accumulated along the way. Clearly some people play at a higher level than others. But within your peer group (and this is key because, frankly, that's your competition), what makes you truly unique? Defining and being able to quickly convey your PVP is a key part of the solution.

Coach Exercise 2: Explaining Your PVP

Take a shot at explaining your PVP to your coach. If you need help getting started, consider the following questions:

1. *If you were a product/service, what would your packaging say about you? Stay away from generic descriptors – everyone is hard-working. Well, almost everyone …*
2. *What qualities or services do people think of when they pick up the phone to call you?*
3. *Does this request align with what people currently say about you and your "personal brand"? If unsure, ask.*

Quick Tip

Having a recognizable PVP is a tricky thing. As we move through our careers we often have so many experiences and learning points it's difficult to decide what to highlight. But that decision is critical. **After all, people don't remember what you've done. They only remember what you've promoted (if you're lucky), and then only what you've promoted most recently.** Your PVP, in its most basic form, is what people know and say about you.

In some cases this PVP equates to a tangible skill, e.g., Tom is the idea guy, Sally is the data guru, or Deb is the marketing whiz who can put a refreshing spin on anything. In other cases one's PVP has more to do with a feeling. It's not only about what you do, but the impact you have and how you make others feel while providing that service.

Defining Your Personality Traits

"Knowing oneself is the greatest knowledge."
—Savita Tyagi

There are plenty of excellent personality assessments on the market that have been validated over decades of study. These include such tools as the Myers-Briggs Type Indicator (MBTI), the Personal Style Indicator (PSI), and the DISC assessment. Some enable an individual to score and interpret their own results, while others require a trained facilitator certified to debrief the test taker.

In this section we will focus on personality as it pertains to the work environment – specifically, job selection and career moves. After all, personality is a key driver for our actions. One's ability to interact with and influence others, handle pressure, manage conflict, etc. can affect the choices made and the risks taken.

Most people seek pleasure and avoid pain. Interestingly, when it comes to the work environment, we all assign different meanings to the extremes. For example, while Person A may view public speaking as a fate worse than death (and many people do!), Person B may see it as an opportunity to showcase his or her talents, a chance to advance, or even a job perk.

Knowing what you enjoy and want in a job is the first step. Getting the role you seek is, of course, the ultimate goal. Typically, people who have jobs that complement their personalities are happier and more fulfilled. Many employers understand the value of aligning worker interests with the required tasks, as satisfied employees are more productive and customer-focused, have greater engagement, and are sick much less frequently than those without a sense of fulfillment. Many forward-thinking organizations provide employees with assessment tools such as this book to arrive at a mutually beneficial outcome.

Self-Guided Exercise 1: Leveraging Your Personality

The following three-step exercise will help you identify the personal qualities that will make you a success in the eyes of your current manager, headhunter, or internal staffing professional.

Step 1: Isolating Your Personality Traits

Read the list of qualities below and circle those that best describe you. If you are unsure if a term truly describes you, do not circle it. Reserve circles for those descriptors with which you most clearly identify. Additional space is provided for you to write other qualities that may describe you better or differentiate you from other professionals, colleagues, or job seekers.

Common Personality Traits			
Accessible	Active	Adaptable	Appreciative
Articulate	Balanced	Brilliant	Challenging
Charismatic	Conscientious	Courageous	Creative
Decisive	Dedicated	Disciplined	Eloquent
Flexible	Focused	Genuine	Humble
Humorous	Idealistic	Imaginative	Impressive
Independent	Innovative	Insightful	Intelligent
Intuitive	Logical	Lovable	Loyal
Methodical	Objective	Observant	Organized
Original	Passionate	Patient	Perceptive
Perfectionist	Personable	Persuasive	Polished
Practical	Precise	Principled	Prudent
Punctual	Rational	Realistic	Resourceful
Respectful	Responsible	Self-reliant	Shrewd
Stoic	Systematic	Thorough	Understanding

Step 2: Prune and Prioritize Your List

Of the qualities you circled, which do you think describe you the best? List the top five in the chart below.

My Top 5 Personality Traits
Rank: 1
Rank: 2
Rank: 3
Rank: 4
Rank: 5

Step 3: Describe Your Traits

For each of the traits listed above, write a few sentences describing a time when you displayed the characteristic. Your example does not have to be work-related, but that is preferred.

Note: Do not skip this step. In Phase 2, "Building a Rock Star Resume," these examples will serve as the foundation for your key accomplishments. See the example below:

Sample Trait 1 Resourceful

Example: I recently demonstrated resourcefulness by avoiding costly printing and mailing expenses by repurposing a legacy customer brochure to a more useful and dynamic web-based marketing vehicle during a crucial project implementation.

Now you try it!

Trait 1
Example:

Trait 2
Example
Trait 3
Example:

If you have trouble coming up with at least one example of each personality trait, consider whether your assessment answers accurately reflected who you are. Sometimes when answering assessments, participants are tempted to portray who they *wish to be* rather than who they *currently are*. Be sure to keep yourself in the "HOT seat," and be Honest, Objective and Thorough throughout. There is nothing wrong with knowing where you want to go – in your career and as a person – but that is a *development* plan. For now, we are focusing on you in the "as is" state.

Uncovering Your Interests

Personality + Interests = Choice of Route to Goal

Obviously, people's interests vary tremendously. Some enjoy artistic endeavors such as writing or graphic design. Others prefer competitive sports or sales. Still others prefer the challenge that comes from numerical manipulation or computing. If you secure a position that is in line with your interests, the chances that you will enjoy and expand your career increase.

In the past, companies frowned upon those who, in their subjective assessment, changed jobs frequently. These days, many hiring managers are beginning to soften their attitude. Given the volatility of many organizations, the economic turmoil of the past few years, and the wealth of opportunities available to top-tier performers, it is more common in today's work environment. Top-tier professionals are self-directed mobile commodities who manage their careers the way an entrepreneur manages a business. In fact, staying "too long" at one organization, especially without appropriate advancement, can be viewed as a sign of complacency or a stalled career.

Of course, sometimes the choice to change jobs is not up to us. Sometimes we fall victim to downsizing, restructuring, or other events that are outside our control and have little to with our performance. I call this the **corporate pronoun phenomenon**. It's when someone says, in essence: "*We* did this. *We* did that. *They* fired *me*."

Regardless of what prompted the move, it's important to manage the message. After all, although frequent moves are more commonplace these days, there is something to be said for stability. If you bounce to a new job every other year it will raise eyebrows. By actively monitoring your interests, you can manage both planned and unforeseen job changes to help ensure only productive moves are made.

Remember: career changes should never be made out of desperation.

Self-Guided Exercise 2: Leveraging Your Interests

The following is a list of work-related activities. Check the corresponding boxes to note your current level of interest. Once again, additional space has been provided should you wish to record other interests.

Step 1: Highlighting Your Interests

Interests are not skills. You may be interested in trying a task that you have yet to explore professionally. This is a common desire and can sometimes be accommodated in a job change. For example, if you are a marketing manager who is interested in selling, you may seek a position that focuses primarily on marketing, but also features a sales component. It's important to keep track of these job wish-list factors, but for this exercise, focus on only those items for which you currently have at least some aptitude.

The Introvert's Guide to Job Hunting

Competency Topic	No Interest 0	Some Interest 1	Strong Interest 2
Pricing			
Negotiating			
Problem solving			
Project management			
Investigating/researching			
Concept creation/idea generation			
Creating new products/services			
Product or service promotion			
Team-based work			
Teaching/training			
Leading/motivating			
Selling/persuading			
Public speaking			
Writing			
Managing			
Computer programming			
Software design			
Data tracking			
Financial analysis			
Consulting			
Problem solving			

Step 2: Prune and Prioritize Your List

Of the interests noted, which have the strongest pull for you? Keep in mind that you should have an aptitude for them. List and rank the top five in the chart below.

My Top 5 Interests
Rank: 1
Rank: 2
Rank: 3
Rank: 4
Rank: 5

Coach Exercise 3: Knowing What You Don't Want

*You should also pay attention to those items that you have no interest in at all. Are they needed in your current job? Will they be needed in your dream job? Discuss this with your career coach. As you do, be sure to explore your **personal nonnegotiable** items. These might include amount of travel, location of role, or other items that fly in the face of your vision, values, or desires.*

An Example of a Nonnegotiable

Early in my career I had a manager who I really respected. Not only was he a competent professional and an excellent mentor, he was an all-around nice guy. The trouble was (at least from my perspective), he wasn't rising fast enough in the organization. He was a bright guy and a dedicated worker, but never seemed to get into the "in crowd" – the supposedly nonexistent circle of preference that often "breaks the ties" when it comes to talent reviews or succession-plan-based promotions.

I had a feeling that, in his case, this was due to a lack of visibility. He wasn't a drinker so the happy-hour crowd often went neglected. And as an introvert, he naturally shied away from the "optional" social gatherings that help one build relationships. Taken by themselves, these are not insurmountable obstacles. Clearly you don't have to be a boozehound or a social butterfly to succeed at work. But he also had the habit of leaving every day at four-thirty. However, he was in the office at six a.m. (an action that no one saw) and was online working late in the evening. I suspect, however, that the thing that stuck in people's minds was his early departure.

I asked him about it once and his reply was so honest and straightforward it actually changed my perspective on work–life balance.

"Tim," he said, "when I was a boy, my father was never around. He was a good man – don't get me wrong – but the lure of chasing a lifestyle and the pressure of supporting a large family kept him away from us most of the time. He was a good provider, but I never really got to know the man.

"You know, I have five kids myself, and I was determined not to make the same mistakes. So I made a deal with the family that (travel and emergencies aside) I'd be home for dinner four nights per week minimum.

"I've missed an opportunity or two because of the practice, but it's a nonnegotiable for me. I don't regret it, and if you'd seen my kids you'd know exactly why."

This is the kind of stuff that doesn't show up on resumes or talent reviews, but it's what makes a person truly special. All things being equal, I'd hire a person with this level of character over a face-time jockey any day. Character counts – you just have to make it visible.

I kept in touch with the guy over the years and am happy to report that not only is he thriving at work, but now that his kids are in college and "off the payroll," he's shifted gears and has actually taken a much more senior role in a different part of the world. It's all about what's important.

Personality/Interest Research

Obviously the exercises noted above (and those that follow) are dependent on the reader's perceptions and understanding of themselves and their true goals. Keen self-awareness combined with feedback from others is, in my view, the most effective and practical way to obtain clarity on goals and move toward their achievement.

While some people fall victim to circumstance and/or rely solely on innate talent to succeed, I prefer instead to leverage the controllable forces of perspective and persistence. Those characteristics, when combined with personal creativity and innovation, can help anyone achieve success in a chosen endeavor. If you or your organization is interested in a practical example of this process, log on to www.plotlineleadership.com for details of my keynote presentation "Power Through: How to Leverage Perspective and Persistence."

There are a number of time-tested research studies in this area that can help increase your self-knowledge. One such test, developed by psychologist John L. Holland, is the Theory of Career Choice (RIASEC). It maintains that people prefer jobs in which they can be around others who are like them. Holland asserts that people search for environments that will let them use their skills and abilities, and express their attitudes and values, while taking on enjoyable problems and roles.

Holland's theory notes that behavior is determined by an interaction between personality and environment and is centered on the notion that most people fit into one of six personality types:

- **Realistic – Doers**: Enjoy working with their hands, building or fixing things
- **Investigative – Thinkers**: Enjoy researching, investigating, or solving problems
- **Artistic – Creators:** Enjoy creating or designing things
- **Social – Helpers:** Enjoy helping others through various endeavors, from teaching to healthcare
- **Enterprising – Persuaders:** Enjoy leading and influencing others
- **Conventional – Organizers:** Enjoy procedures, working with numbers, or planning

If given the opportunity, be it through your current job or self-study, I'd encourage you to take part in one of these assessments. No single assessment can completely capture the essence of an individual, but collectively they can provide pieces of the puzzle that will help you navigate to the best possible career position.

Highlighting Your Skills

Now that you have a broad career goal based on your personality and interests, it is time to ask yourself if you have the skills required of a marketable candidate.

We all have different skill sets – from editing to architecture, from data entry to data analysis. Having a realistic understanding of what you do well and what you need to develop can provide a distinct advantage in the workplace. When you are aware of your skills you can seek job opportunities that capitalize on these strengths. This awareness also provides the insight needed to partner with those who can do what you cannot.

Skills require training and experience to develop. You can acquire skills through on-the-job training, formal classes, volunteer activities, informal learning, mentoring programs, or outside interests. Understand, though, that deliberate and focused effort is a requirement for skill enhancement. Simply having an aptitude in a particular area will rarely be sufficient under the pressure of the work environment.

In any case, to advance your career you must be able to describe your skills to the hiring manager and give concrete reasons why they would be of value in the new role. Understanding the areas of skill concentration is the first step in this process.

Self-Guided Exercise 3: Leveraging Your Skills

Take a few moments to rate each of the skills in the six categories listed below.

Step 1: Rate Your Skills

Use the following rating system to fill in the chart below:

- Little or no skill   = 0
- Some skill   = 1
- High skill   = 2

Group 1	Rating	Group 2	Rating
Mediation/team interventions		Developing a vision	
Crafting proposals/presentations		Designing a strategy	
Writing/editing		Motivating others	
Public speaking		Selling/influencing	
Negotiating		Conflict resolution	
Service/product/person promotion		Succeeding through systems	
Training		Idea generation	
Total =		**Total =**	

Group 3	Rating	Group 4	Rating
Questioning current state		Financial analysis	
Researching alternatives		Budgeting/expense reporting	
Testing hypotheses		Vendor management	
Investigating root-cause issues		ROI analysis	
Designing new approaches		Forecasting	
Reviewing results		"Big data" manipulation	
Assessments		Statistical analysis	
Total =		Total =	
Group 5	Rating	Group 6	Rating
Project management		Computer programming	
Conducting performance reviews		Audio/visual operations	
Team-based problem solving		Installing equipment	
Delegating		Demonstrating equipment	
Career coaching		Data manipulation	
Succeeding through others		Fixing office hardware	
Mentoring		Website design	
Total =		Total =	

Step 2: Assess Your Results

Compile your findings by recording the totals for each skill group below. The group with the highest score gives an indication of your greatest skill set. Don't get caught up in the different labels, as the categories are designed to provide a general area of interest. We will soon dive into more specific details.

Group	Score	Relates to:
1		Communication/Creative Skills
2		Leadership Skills
3		Analytical/Consultative Skills
4		Quantitative Skills
5		Managerial Skills
6		Technical Skills

Step 3: Prune and Prioritize Your List

Look again at the information you recorded in Step 1. Of the skills you noted, which are your strongest? List and rank the top five in the chart below according to both the individual skill and its corresponding group.

My Top 5 Skills		
Ranking	Skill	Group
Example:	Crafting proposals	Communications/Creative
1		
2		
3		
4		
5		

Defining Your Personal and Work Values

Now it's time to ask yourself if you believe *in the goal you are pursuing.*

Your work life will be unfulfilling if the organization or the people who lead it run counter to your values and beliefs. While you may not be able to get a true sense of the work environment before accepting a position in a new company, you can certainly acquire an understanding of the corporate culture. More important, if you understand and commit to paper that which you hold in the highest regard, you will be better prepared to act if you encounter something outside the scope of your values and what you deem acceptable in a position.

Self-Guided Exercise 4: Leveraging Your Values

The following will help you isolate and analyze your personal and career values. Space has been provided for you to add other descriptors.

Step 1: Rank Your Values

Rank the personal and work-related values below from 1 to 10, with 1 being the most important. Extra space is provided in each category so that you can substitute more meaningful concepts.

Personal Values	Rank	Work Values	Rank
Good health and vitality		Independent work	
Respect from peers		Financial gain	
Marriage, family, and friends		Creativity	
Independence		Flexible hours, environment	
Financial security		Secure job	
Quality/safe surroundings		Many activities/problem solving	
Leisure time		Helping others	

Physical activity		Team-based work	
Volunteer work		Managing/leading	
Creative time		Respect from coworkers	

Step 2: Prune and Prioritize Your List

Of the values you noted, which are your strongest? List and rank the top five in the chart below.

My Top 5 Values		
	Personal	Work
Rank: 1		
Rank: 2		
Rank: 3		
Rank: 4		
Rank: 5		

It's important that these two sets of values align and support what you want to accomplish. Remember, most of us spend a tremendous amount of time working. But even if your job requires more traditional hours, any part of your life spent in conflict with your values will bear a heavy price.

A Personal Summary

At this point you should have a good understanding of your personal attributes, interests, skills, and values.

Self-Guided Exercise 5: Drafting Your Personal Summary

Take a moment to reflect on what you have learned. If someone were to ask you (say during an interview): "How would you describe yourself?" what answer would you provide? In the space below, describe yourself in a few short sentences. Be sure to note what is important to you and how that might fit with what they need in a given role.

Note: Your answer will serve as the foundation for the Professional Summary you will craft in the next phase – "Building a Rock Star Resume."

Personal Summary

_____

_____

_____

_____

_____

_____

_____

_____

_____

_____

Congratulations! You're ready to move on to Part 2.

Part 2: Career Knowledge Evaluation

To obtain success in any profession you need to arm yourself with knowledge that can help you navigate your desired career path. In the last section you examined your interests, skills, and values in broad, personal terms. Now you'll have the opportunity to refine your focus and analyze your work self in terms of the following five **career knowledge success factors:**

1. Self Knowledge – Establishing Your Personal Value Proposition (PVP)
2. Colleague Knowledge – Securing an Informal 360
3. Organizational Awareness – Ensuring the Right Fit
4. Development Options – Expanding Your Possibilities
5. Career Plan – Defining the Path to Goal

To ensure the effectiveness of the assessment, remember to be a HOT property: Honest, Objective, and Thorough. If you are employed, think of the assessment in terms of your current role. If you are in transition, think of the assessment in terms of your most recent work experience.

Self-Guided Exercise 6: Understanding Career Success Factors

The following exercise lists a series of statements that will measure your current standing in terms of five **career knowledge success factors** *and fifteen underlying building blocks.*

Step 1: Rate the Relative Truth of Each Statement

Rate the truth of each statement from 1 to 4 according to your career management activities to date.

> 1 = **Disagree** – No work on the activity done to date
> 2 = **Partially Agree** – Planned/explored the activity
> 3 = **Agree** – Activity is in process with some results
> 4 = **Completely Agree** – Activity is complete

Sample Questions	Rating
I have at least two non-work-related interests or hobbies at which I excel. (Think current job.)	3
I can explain how these interests complement or could potentially enhance my effectiveness in current/future roles.	2
I can list several work-related projects that interest me – even if they fall outside my current responsibilities.	4
I have taken steps to pursue projects at work that interest me.	1
I am aware of the aspects of my role and other potential jobs that I do not enjoy.	2

Step 2: Record and Compare Your Answers

1. Transfer your responses according to question number as shown. (Note: You will complete this for items 6-15 as well.)

Question Numbers   **Building Blocks   Success Factor**

1. **3**   2. **2**   3. **4**   4. **1**   5. **2**   Interests ___
6. ___   7. ___   8. ___   9. ___   10. ___   Skills ___   Work Self __
11. ___   12. ___   13. ___   14. ___   15. ___   Values ___

2. Add across the rows to determine your Building Block scores.

Question Numbers   **Building Blocks   Success Factor**

1. **3**   2. **2**   3. **4**   4. **1**   5. **2**   Interests _12__
6. ___   7. ___   8. ___   9. ___   10. ___   Skills ___   Work Self __
11. ___   12. ___   13. ___   14. ___   15. ___   Values ___

3. Add the three Building Blocks in each category to determine your Success Factor score.

Question Numbers					Building Blocks	Success Factor
1. **3**	2. **2**	3. **4**	4. **1**	5. **2**	Interests _12__	
6. ___	7. ___	8. ___	9. ___	10. ___	Skills _e.g. 16__	Work Self _43_
11. ___	12. ___	13. ___	14. ___	15. ___	Values _e.g.15__	

Step 3: Gain Perspective

To interpret your scores, use the following guidelines:

- A Building Block score of 12 or more is considered average.
- A Success Factor score of 36 is considered average.

As you begin to look at your scores, don't hyper-focus on your lower numbers. No one is perfect at everything. That isn't to say you should ignore your weak points. It's important to make sure current deficiencies or "development opportunities" don't swell into "career derailers" – things that can stall your career or knock you off course. However, most people obtain success by leveraging their strengths. Begin by focusing on what you do well and how you can capitalize on those areas.

Finally, read the descriptions of each Building Block and Success Factor. The explanations will offer valuable information about specific steps you can take to further your career satisfaction and growth in these areas. Once you have finished, discuss each with your career coach.

To achieve success you must decide where you stand ... and then stand up.

Success Factor 1: Self Knowledge

Questionnaire

Do you agree with the statement? Rate from 1 to 4 **1** = Disagree, **2** = Partially Agree – Activity planned, **3** = Agree – Activity in process, **4** = Completely Agree – Complete	
Question	**Rating**
1. I have at least two non-work-related interests or hobbies at which I excel. (Think current job.)	
2. I can explain how these interests complement or could potentially enhance my effectiveness in current/future roles.	
3. I can list several work-related projects that interest me – even if they fall outside my current responsibilities.	
4. I have taken steps to pursue projects at work that interest me.	
5. I am aware of the aspects of my role and other potential jobs that I do not enjoy.	
6. I have the communication skills required to build relationships with colleagues.	
7. I have made my accomplishments known to others without being boastful.	
8. I am aware of my strengths and weaknesses as they pertain to my current job.	
9. I have the interpersonal savvy required to rally support and secure skills via others that complement my shortcomings.	
10. I have a habit of *doing what I say I will do*, have taken action on past development plans, and can list the new skills I have acquired as a result.	
11. I know what motivates me and keeps me engaged at work.	
12. I can describe how these factors align with and support my values.	
13. I can describe how my current job complements or causes conflict with my values.	

Do you agree with the statement? Rate from 1 to 4	
1 = Disagree, **2** = Partially Agree – Activity planned, **3** = Agree – Activity in process, **4** = Completely Agree – Complete	
14. I have a firm commitment to my values and clearly understand my nonnegotiables in terms of work/life balance.	
15. To enhance my engagement and productivity, I've discussed these drivers with my manager.	

Question Numbers   **Building Blocks Success Factor**

1. ___   2. ___   3. ___   4. ___   5. ___   Interests ___

6. ___   7. ___   8. ___   9. ___   10. ___   Skills ___   Work Self ___

11. ___   12. ___   13. ___   14. ___   15. ___   Values ___

Success Factor 1: Self Knowledge

Jobs are relatively easy to come by. Finding, nurturing, and flourishing in a career you love is another matter entirely. To achieve that which eludes the average person, you must be willing to do above-average things. This means taking stock of your interests, skills, and values. An understanding of your work-related characteristics will allow you to seek every opportunity to capitalize on the features that make you unique.

As you read each section, reflect on how you scored. Focus on ways to improve your weak spots and making your strengths even more powerful.

Interests

People are inquisitive by nature. Having a career that allows you to explore your interests makes the day shorter. The hours will fly by.

Self-Guided Exercise 7: Your Ideal Day

In the space below, craft an ideal day at work. Be as descriptive as you can. Include how and when you would get to work, the activities you would perform, and a description of the people you would interact with while there.

Your Ideal Day

_____

_____

_____

_____

_____

Though you may not attain your dream position right away, you can certainly pull aspects of that job into your current situation. What's more, if your current position is nothing like the job you just described, you may want to consider a more drastic career move. Understand that satisfaction in the workplace is of primary importance. It is very difficult to spend forty to sixty hours per week doing something for which you have no passion, especially in the long term.

> **Bonus Points:** *Do you already have the ideal job in mind? If you've started to look at positions online, take a few minutes to jot down, in the space below, the specific elements of the job description that you find most appealing.*

Job Description Analysis

_____

_____

_____

_____

_____

Remember not to be afraid of job descriptions. The reality is that most organizations don't make active or productive use of the tools once people are hired – that's why they often include the phrase "and other duties as assigned." It's a catchall – a way to ensure needs are covered without being locked into specifics.

While there may be items that are truly representative of minimum qualifications, e.g., years of experience or education, most items represent a wish list of skills and experiences. If you present a good case (depending on the talent market, economy, and geography) you can often snag a job without having all items on the list. Just be sure you have meaningful substitutes, e.g., certifications and experience instead of formal degrees and additional skills/experiences to make up for the shortfall.

Skills

As we saw in Part 1, a skill is an ability or behavior used to produce a definitive result. Now that you have identified your skills, you should begin to seek ways of improving those that you will need most urgently, i.e., on your current or next job. By consistently expanding and honing your skill set, you will increase your career options and ensure that you are ready to pounce when opportunities present themselves. Such actions may also cause your current employers to notice your enthusiasm and ambition and will help further your career in the current organization.

Values

Our values act as an internal compass. They shape our attitudes and influence the way we interact and communicate with others. When our work life is in harmony with our values we feel content. When work is at odds with our values, we experience stress and intrapersonal conflict. Knowing your values and the key "hot spots" that support or undermine them is crucial to career success. The following is a good rule of thumb:

If you love what you do but are unhappy with your company, colleagues, or manager, you probably need a **job change***.*

If you enjoy your working environment but dread doing the work, you probably need a **career change***.*

Success Factor 2: Colleague Knowledge

Questionnaire

Do you agree with the statement? Rate 1 to 4 **1** = Disagree, **2** = Partially Agree – Activity planned, **3** = Agree – Activity in process, **4** = Completely Agree – Complete	
Question	**Rating**
1. I have a productive working relationship with my manager and know what it takes to meet and exceed expectations for my role.	
2. I seek specific, timely, measureable feedback from my manager regarding my performance.	
3. I routinely ask my manager (and mentor as appropriate) for coaching suggestions on how to improve my performance.	
4. I know the topics my manager would earmark as my development areas.	
5. I take full advantage of formal performance reviews by requesting feedback on my work style and results.	
6. I can list the skills I have, the behaviors I demonstrate, and the competencies I possess that are most valued by my coworkers.	
7. I know the impression I make on my colleagues and have eliminated blind spots.	
8. I have discussed my performance with my peers, including feedback obtained via any 360 or other assessment (preserving confidentially as needed).	
9. I am open to and have made an effort to adopt the performance improvement suggestions offered by my coworkers.	
10. I know and have improved the weaknesses noted by my colleagues and have addressed their criticisms where valid.	
11. I act as an ambassador for my department, use social media wisely, and filter formal inquires to appropriate channels within the organization.	
12. I know what is and is not important to my internal customers.	

Do you agree with the statement? Rate 1 to 4 **1** = Disagree, **2** = Partially Agree – Activity planned, **3** = Agree – Activity in process, **4** = Completely Agree – Complete	
13. I am aware of potential areas of conflict and work to create mutual wins.	
14. I routinely ask for feedback from internal customers.	
15. I know what impression I make on people outside my work group in the long and short term.	

Question Numbers   **Building Blocks**   **Success Factor**

1. ___   2. ___   3. ___   4. ___   5. ___   Manager ___

6. ___   7. ___   8. ___   9. ___   10. ___   Coworkers ___   ___ Colleagues

11. ___   12. ___   13. ___   14. ___   15. ___   Internal Partners ___

Success Factor 2: Colleague Knowledge

"A dream that has no people in it isn't much of a dream."
—Ray Melillo

No matter what profession you choose, interactions with the people in your work environment will play a critical role in how effectively you perform and how quickly you advance. This concept goes far beyond networking. It involves the mutually beneficial coaching and mentoring relationships that you develop with others.

Gathering feedback, evaluating the input, and designing a plan to put the constructive ideas to work are not easy tasks. Many organizations spend impressive sums conducting formal 360 assessments for segments of their workforce. However, much of the same information can be acquired through thoughtful interaction with those around you.

Sometimes this informal data gathering is even more effective than traditional 360s as some participants shy away from giving negative or even constructive feedback in the latter setting. This is especially true in cases where the 360 has an impact on performance evaluations. There is a place for formal instruments, to be sure, but sometimes you just need a quick read on what you do well and whether you have any proverbial broccoli stuck in your teeth. Consider the following sources of input as you seek feedback.

Manager

Obviously your manager is an important source of feedback regarding your performance. Many companies conduct annual or even quarterly performance appraisals. These documents are critical, especially when compared to each other over time. When examining your reviews, look for trends in both strengths and weakness.

The quality of projects given to you is another powerful indicator of your manager's faith in your ability. If you are consistently being asked to sponsor projects, lead teams, or run meetings, you are likely on the right track. If you're tasked with support work, it could be a red flag. Now that you know what to look for, begin to use that information to enhance or alter your work habits. If you need to, request time to discuss these issues with your manager.

Colleagues

Let's face it: there is a healthy (and sometimes not-so-healthy) spirit of competition among colleagues, especially those working in the same department. This can be shockingly overt. For example, while working in India I was surprised to learn that employees would routinely compare paychecks in the hallway to ensure bonuses, merit increases, and promotional adjustments were in line with expectations.

In other cases (most applicable to U.S. readers) the comparisons and competition are more covert in nature. At its worst this can degrade into passive-aggressive behavior. Most often, however, it presents itself in harmless and, frankly, understandable water-cooler chat during which you might overhear someone say, for example: "Why did *so-and-so* get the promotion? He's a slacker."

In short, colleagues keep tabs on each other and can often sense when something is out of whack. This can have serious implications for the health of an organization and the engagement of its employees. For the job seeker, however, it's a good phenomenon to be aware of and use to your advantage.

Colleagues know your style and competency level, and have watched how you've handled your current position over an extended period. They can provide a vital view of how you communicate, handle stress, and come across on a daily basis. Depending on how closely you interact, the feedback obtained from your colleagues can be critical to your continued improvement. While you can certainly acquire this information on an informal basis, you may want to set up formal feedback exchange sessions. Just be prepared to return the favor.

Internal Partners

An excellent way to validate or call into question the views presented by your manager and colleagues is to compare them with the opinions of those outside your department with whom you have worked – especially internal customers. You can gain similar input by contacting external customers, vendors, or colleagues from previous positions and asking them for an objective analysis of your style and performance.

Securing an objective outside view is critical. In some cases it can balance a person's overly optimistic view of his or her value and current contribution level to the organization. In others, it can provide a much-needed confidence-boosting pat on the back. Tough though it may be, always try to be thoughtful and balanced when "reviewing your own press." Heed the messages provided in trends, but don't let a single voice build you up or knock you down.

Success Factor 3: Organizational Awareness

Questionnaire

Do you agree with the statement? Rate 1 to 4 **1** = Disagree, **2** = Partially Agree – Activity planned, **3** = Agree – Activity in process, **4** = Completely Agree – Complete	
Question	**Rating**
1. I understand my organization's structure, mission, vision, and strategy.	
2. I understand the role my department plays in driving the success of the organization's strategy.	
3. I know the key decision makers in my functional area and am aware of their goals for my department.	
4. I can explain my company's strategic direction and how I can contribute.	
5. I understand the formal policies that affect my plans for advancement.	
6. I have internal connections that allow me to effectively circumvent duplicative or unnecessary procedures without breaking the rules.	
7. I know who to call on to get things done quickly and/or gain project approval – whose yes means yes and whose no means no.	
8. I can describe my company's informal promotion practices and know how to navigate them.	
9. I know what my manager and other top performers do to achieve results.	
10. I have influential connections in other departments that can help cut through bureaucratic red tape.	
11. I stay abreast of best practices and new developments in my field via reading, conferences, etc.	
12. I am aware of the potential threats and uncertainties presented by our competition, including nontraditional competitors.	

Do you agree with the statement? Rate 1 to 4 **1** = Disagree, **2** = Partially Agree – Activity planned, **3** = Agree – Activity in process, **4** = Completely Agree – Complete	
13. I understand how the government, economy, and other external forces affect my manager's decisions as well as company polices.	
14. I can list traditional and "blue ocean" opportunities for my company in the near future.	
15. I know our organizational strengths and weaknesses and how they set us up to deal with the future.	

Question Numbers   **Building Blocks**   **Success Factor**

1. ___   2. ___   3. ___   4. ___   5. ___   Formal Structure ___
6. ___   7.___   8.___   9.___   10.___   Informal Structure___   __ Org. Awareness
11.___   12.__   13.___   14.___   15.___   Strategic Goals ___

Success Factor 3: Organizational Awareness

Home-field advantage is sought after in sports. Sharp competitors know the value of playing in a familiar setting. Having a clear understanding of your organization's formal policies, informal practices, and strategic needs is a lot like having home-field advantage at work. You can use that knowledge to gain a competitive edge over both external candidates and less savvy internal colleagues who would challenge you for promotions.

Formal Career Path Structure

These are the formal rules of the game – the official playbook: If you are seeking a role within your current organization, it's critical that you take time to understand formal human resource practices such as the job-posting and application process, promotion rules and requirements, career ladders and pathing, talent reviews and succession planning practices, available training programs and development options, the organization framework applicable to your designed role, and other polices that govern how companies manage talent and conduct business.

The more you know about this playbook the better versed you will be to navigate your career and make the best possible choices. It can also give you a better negotiating position should you decide to look at external options. For example, if your organization requires you to be in the role for one year before applying for a new opportunity and a competitor comes calling with an attractive offer, knowing the rules can help you decide whether to apply for an exception or make the leap. Make it a point to study your organization's formal talent-management practices. Knowledge can come from HR or your network. You do have a network, don't you?

Informal Career-Path Structure

This is what *actually* happens as the game is played. Think of them as the "house rules." They include unwritten policies, cultural norms, and unofficial practices that shape people's actions. While hiring managers rarely seek to overtly circumvent HR policies, it's naive to think that "gentleman's agreements" don't exist.

For example, hiring managers sometimes post roles internally only because they must fulfill a legal obligation or company requirement. While they may put you through the motions to comply with the *formal* practice, sometimes an external candidate or internal applicant has already been selected. Similar situations can apply to performance reviews, talent reviews, and succession planning. For example, managers who are under pressure to hit performance distribution or "Ready Now" replacement-planning objectives may send one message with a tick-box exercise and another with their actions. I had a colleague who was consistently rated high in both performance and talent review scores and knew through back channels that she was on a succession list for a VP role, but nothing ever came of it. It turned out that she was used as a placeholder to meet the replacement-plan quota, but was never in serious contention for a VP spot.

To be effective at work, and by association in your career planning, you need to understand and effectively navigate the informal career-path structure of your company, division, department, and team. Doing so will dramatically enhance the power of your network and your ability to rise in the organization.

Strategic Goals and Outlook

Just as the weather, fans, and officials affect the pace of the game and the strategy of the teams, a variety of internal and external forces affect the way companies operate. Understanding both the organization's strategic goals and how external forces affect your company is critical to your career success. After all, what good is it to be perfectly prepared for a challenging project if the company plans to lay-off or sell the entire division due to tumultuous economic conditions?

Savvy career planners will have at least a working knowledge of their organization's strategic plan and understand how it affects their department and, ultimately, their role in the company. If you are early in your career or in a role that seems too far removed from the strategic designs of a large organization, consider the strategic or operational plans for your department.

The following questions provide a framework for understanding the external environment your company faces:

- Is the company facing any mergers or acquisitions?
- Are layoffs looming? If so, in what area?
- Where have sales revenue and profits been over the past year?
- What projects/products are doing well or having trouble?
- How is the government affecting your business?
- Where is the competition beating you? Where are you strong?
- How is new technology shaping/changing your business?

- What positions are being opened by retirements, promotions, or other vacancies?
- Are there any plans to send work offshore?
- Is the organization facing pressure to reduce expenses, particularly in SG&A/overhead functions?

Quick Tip

Resist the temptation to gloss over this section or assume that it doesn't apply to you. Every organization values different roles differently. For example, in some companies, HR or IT is a valued part of the business with a visible seat at the leadership table. In others, it's regarded as a basic necessity or, worse, a necessary evil that should be outsourced. Savvy professionals will have a good grasp of not only the health of the company and the external forces that can affect it, but also how their particular department is perceived.

There is no point climbing a dead tree.

It requires additional effort, but increasing your organizational awareness can help you:

- Confirm or call into question the health of your company
- Provide a framework for having a meaningful business conversation with your manager
- Gauge your prospects for advancement
- Assess the standing of your department
- Prepare for meaningful conversations with other organizations – ensuring the external job sought is worth the effort.

To learn more about strategic planning, pick up a copy of my book *Strategic Planning Unleashed* or log on to www.plotlineleadership.com.

Success Factor 4: Development Options

Questionnaire

Do you agree with the statement? Rate 1 to 4 1 = Disagree, 2 = Partially Agree – Activity planned, 3 = Agree – Activity in process, 4 = Completely Agree – Complete	
Question	**Rating**
1. I know of several projects within my current role that I could take on to expand my skills and/or reduce deficiencies.	
2. I know of projects outside my current job description that I could take on to expand my skills while leveraging core strengths.	
3. I consistently streamline my work processes to save time for learning.	
4. I maintain excellent performance in my role and routinely ask for additional assignments.	
5. I know how my work and special projects help the organization.	
6. I am a student of my profession and continuously learn with an eye toward future opportunities.	
7. I keep informed about new opportunities in and outside my current company via online networking tools, job sites, and other mediums.	
8. I have a vision of what my next role will look like (even if it's not readily apparent on an org chart).	
9. I have a clear plan for pursuing the next job.	
10. I have discussed this plan with the appropriate people and secured input.	
11. I often talk to people about their jobs to discover what interests me, conducting formal informational interviews as appropriate.	
12. I know of several career opportunities within my current profession/company that I could pursue.	

Do you agree with the statement? Rate 1 to 4 **1** = Disagree, **2** = Partially Agree – Activity planned, **3** = Agree – Activity in process, **4** = Completely Agree – Complete	
13. I have a short list of career opportunities outside my current profession/company that I could pursue.	
14. I have discussed these options with others for an objective view of my potential success.	
15. I have specific evaluation system used to gauge the viability of opportunities outside my main core competency.	

Question Numbers   **Building Blocks**   **Success Factor**

1. ___ 2. ___ 3. ___ 4. ___ 5. ___ Current Job ___
6. ___ 7.___ 8.___ 9.___ 10.___ Next Job ___
11.___ 12.___ 13.___ 14.___ 15.___ Career Opportunities ___

Development Options ___

Success Factor 4: Development Options

"Success occurs when opportunity and preparedness meet."
- Zig Ziglar

It's important to have a clear definition of "career development." While some consider development the chance to work on new initiatives, manage people, lead projects, or even take an international assignment, in many employees' minds career development is code for promotion. There's nothing wrong with that; it's just important to be honest about what you really want and expect from your current organization. Even within the *promotion* frame of reference there are differences. For some, a new title is critical. For others, titles matter little in the face of a higher salary and greater bonus. Knowing what you want and being clear on how to ask for it is a critical first step.

Quick Tip

This plays out differently in different parts of the world. I spent a few years living and working as an HR professional in Europe and Asia. During one assignment I was helping to prepare growth regions for expansion by providing advanced training to managerial candidates. During a break in a Singapore-based seminar, a gentleman from India approached me to get a read on his performance.

"I'd really like to be a manager," he said.

Impressed by his interest in the topic, I asked, "What excites you about the possibility – is it the opportunity to develop staff, deliver results through others, have more influence over company projects …?"

"Actually," he said, "I'm hoping to get married."

My confusion must have crossed the cultural divide, because he quickly went on to explain that in that part of the world having a managerial title was a valuable status symbol – one seen as an important sign of success and future prospects by both family and potential romantic partners.

Being a bit of a socially awkward introvert (always fun during international travel), I asked, "How important is the title?"

He looked around quickly to ensure no one was listening, and said, "Actually, I'd take less money."

This may seem crazy to a Western reader, but that's the point. Development and career management mean different things to different people. As a job seeker, it's important to know what's truly meaningful to you. If, in your new role, you will manage staff (especially international staff), it's critical that you get a true sense of what is important to your direct reports as well. You can't assume that what is important to you is important to them.

Of course, not all career development can involve upward mobility. The higher you rise in an organization the fewer opportunities there are to continue your journey. And with the increasing adoption of flat corporate structures, that reality is becoming more apparent earlier in people's careers. These days, to find fulfillment, gain recognition, and expand your value to the organization, you have to look outside the traditional view of career advancement.

Current Job

Think of your current job as a training camp for your next one. Forget the Peter Principle – the idea that people are allowed to rise to the level of their own incompetence. Sure it happens on occasion, but wise employers and managers aren't going to promote you into a position you aren't ready for ... especially if a poor performance in that position will reflect badly on them. If you want to advance, you will have to be prepared to earn the trust and respect of those for whom you currently work.

Taking on new projects within your current position is an exceptional way to gain new skills and explore diverse interests while demonstrating your effectiveness to your current manager. It can also serve to alleviate some of the boredom and frustration you may be experiencing.

Next Job

The day will come, of course, when you are fully prepared to take on a new position. When an opportunity presents itself you must be ready to strike. Effective career planners will have a prudent strategy for seeking out and applying for a new position. This plan often involves strategic information and the subjective views of your network. When the time comes to make your case, be sure you have sufficient evidence to indicate that you are the perfect choice. Remember that having the support of your current manager can go a long way toward achieving this goal.

Career Opportunities

Depending on your age and interests, or the needs of your organization, you may find yourself seeking opportunities outside of what was once your core competency. This is a natural, fulfilling, and potentially empowering portion of the career lifecycle and should not be feared or avoided. In fact, career changes are more frequent than ever before, with the average person completing two full transitions in his or her lifetime. To be successful in this endeavor you must plan ahead and consider all options. These can include lateral moves to other departments, realigning to a new position of lower status, taking on a new career outside the organization, or even becoming a self-employed consultant.

Bonus Tip for Internal Candidates

Make an attempt to learn about your organization's hiring philosophy. Companies go through phases, usually dependent on who is steering the ship. Sometimes internal talent is valued. Other times, organizations seek new blood and take the position that all fresh ideas will come from outside. Naturally, things are never so black and white. The hiring mix will contain a percentage of both internal and external placements. Still, it's helpful to keep an eye on percentage, especially for top jobs.

Hiring an external person is often more expensive and riskier than opting for a known individual. In theory, this should give you a leg up on the external competition. Some hiring managers will take a risk on a less-qualified internal player with the thought that he or she can leverage an already established internal network to overcome gaps. At the same time, these managers often expect that the external candidate will arrive ready to run.

In either case, it's important to establish a game plan for your entry into the role. If you can expedite your path to break even and begin to contribute value to the company, you will be well on your way to success in the position. Make sure you and your new manager are aligned on what's important in the near and long term.

Success Factor 5: Career Plan

Questionnaire

Do you agree with the statement? Rate 1 to 4 **1** = Disagree, **2** = Partially Agree – Activity planned, **3** = Agree – Activity in process, **4** = Completely Agree – Complete	
Question	**Rating**
1. I take on new projects that support my career goals.	
2. I seek outside sources of information on career development in my field.	
3. I know how my current job is preparing me for future roles.	
4. I know the skills I currently lack for the position I want.	
5. I apply relevant project experiences and skills to my daily work.	
6. I am familiar with the career development procedures and resources within my organization.	
7. I have and meet with a mentor who provides company specific career guidance.	
8. I have networking partners in various departments.	
9. I have intelligent, objective sources of constructive feedback.	
10. I have a productive, open relationship with my manager and coworkers.	
11. I have a training plan and specific objectives approved by my manager.	
12. I take part in all required training programs and apply that knowledge to my job.	
13. I take advantage of my company's internal training resources via its learning management system (LMS) or another medium.	
14. I know and take advantage of the external learning opportunities presented by my company, including executive coaching if offered.	
15. I supplement my training via outside interests, memberships, and activities.	

Question Numbers					Building Blocks	Success Factor
1. ___	2. ___	3. ___	4. ___	5. ___	Informal Development_	
6. ___	7. ___	8. ___	9. ___	10. ___	Internal Partnership ___	___Career Plan
11. ___	12. ___	13. ___	14. ___	15. ___	Formal Training ___	

Success Factor 5: Career Plan

Too much planning can mean too little doing.

Self-analysis and understanding your work environment are critical components of any career plan, but in order for your dreams to become reality, you must take concrete action. Step one involves developing the required experiences and skills to ensure success in your next position. Once acquired, you can leverage your learning and previously developed career network to rally support for your cause.

Many organizations and novice career coaches like to frame development in terms of a 70-20-10 model, which advocates an ideal scenario in which 70 percent of development comes from on-the-job experiences, 20 percent comes from your manager or mentor-led interactions, and the remaining 10 percent comes from formal training. Unfortunately, this practice is based largely on a misunderstanding of the initial research – what it is and what it was intended to point out.

Need a laugh? Ask someone about the origin of the 70-20-10 learning philosophy. Better yet, ask them what it means. The model has slowly become one of those corporate concepts that everyone supports and professes to understand but can't seem to describe with consistency. It's no surprise. Search Google for the term and you'll end up with thousands of articles on how to apply the concept to learning, as well as innovation, product rollouts, and even personal savings.

The idea actually originated through research conducted in the 1980s by Robert Eichinger and Michael Lombardo at the Center for Creative Leadership. While the duo has continued to pontificate on the now globally tested subject in books such as *The Leadership Engine*, the core concept has remained the same.

In short, the researchers asked a pool of successful senior executives to look back on their careers and reflect on where they felt meaningful development came from, i.e., things that made a difference in the way they managed. The results indicated the now-familiar formula:

- 70% on-the-job experiences
- 20% learning from others
- 10% learning from formal courses

The question they asked the executives is, of course, key. It's easy to look at the answer and draw straight-line conclusions about how an organization should tailor its learning approach. Scrap the trainers. Digitize the courseware. And get employees into the field. But not so fast! It's important to consider the context of the question. Remember, this was a look back at events that shaped executives over a career. Is it any surprise that they recalled the people-based interactions?

Think about it. Can you recall the statistics lecture you had in college? What about that PowerPoint presentation you sat through yesterday? No one remembers a textbook. Sure, sometimes people fall in love with concepts, but more frequently they are moved and motivated by other humans. We grow from daily interactions with managers, colleagues, customers, and direct reports. We learn as we do. So what we do in the classroom is critical.

The research also noted the importance of learning from hardships – the personal and professional trials and setbacks one accumulates over a lifetime. While no one would purposefully build such experiences into a development plan, the point about learning from one's mistakes and life lessons should not be overlooked. Getting fired, losing a loved one, and being relocated are all hardships that test your mettle. Typically, people emerge from these trials stronger, wiser, and savvier than before. Those experiences can and should be harnessed where possible.

The ugly truth is that informal "90 percent" is powerful, but amazingly difficult to orchestrate. For example, I learned a lot about crisis management and personal leadership when the engine started sputtering in my two-seat training plane, but that doesn't mean I'd advocate putting high potentials in a dodgy Cessna in hopes of replicating the experience.

The truth is that few organizations have cracked the code on how to successfully scale experiential learning without defaulting to a brutal sink-or-swim approach. Sure, you can put leaders in a classroom, assign mentors, and even invest in a job-rotation program that gives future stars hands-on experience in key departments. However, unless people are taught how to look for and call out coachable moments during those experiences, you'll waste your efforts.

Still, while the accuracy and operational reality of this 70-20-10 is debatable at best, it's an easy way to frame the learning categories and one that you might run into when discussing career options with HR professionals. Regardless of the percentages involved, savvy career planners will consistently leverage all three options.

Informal (Experience-Based) Development

You can gain vital career experience by uncovering and taking part in the informal learning opportunities present in your current job. Savvy career builders are always on the lookout for challenging projects that stretch their skills. Often, these trial-by-fire opportunities present an ideal way for you to experience the next level of work without leaving your current position. Why wait for your dream job to become available when you can begin to pull components of that position into your current work environment?

Internal Partnerships

Unless you are creating a new position or beginning a unique project, chances are someone has done it before. Rather than face the unknown alone, call on your career network. If designed properly, this strong, mutually beneficial group can help you avoid career pitfalls, while speeding you on the way to that next assignment or position. While your current manager may prove most useful in this regard, don't limit yourself. Include others, such as a mentor and respected colleagues, as well as experts from departments in and outside your organization.

Every path paved has been traveled.

I know this may seem odd to the introverted reader, but most people love to talk about themselves. (Actually, you may already know and be exhausted by this.) One way to use this tendency to your advantage and gain some practical interviewing experience in a low-stress environment is to schedule "path to success" conversations with professionals who are in roles that you aspire to.

Ideally, you would *interview* professionals at various stages of their careers to see what life is really like – the unfiltered day to day – in that career. The lessons can be eye-opening. For example, while a junior consulting role may seem exciting when you are in your twenties (despite the workload), given the pay, resume-building experiences, and travel, it can seem less appealing when you have a family and are faced with those responsibilities and the reality of an up-or-out environment.

Take time to benefit from others' experiences by framing some thoughtful questions for those who have gone before you. Examples include:
- What initially attracted you to the profession?
- What are the biggest benefits that come from this career?
- What are the biggest tradeoffs/disappointments?
- What most surprised you about your career path?
- Anything you wished you would have done differently?
- Any free advice?

Success leaves clues. Failure leaves roadmaps.

Formal Training

Perhaps the easiest way to acquire new knowledge and skills is to take part in your company's training programs. Most organizations offer a variety of learning opportunities, including instructor-led classes, recorded online trainings, and real-time video seminars. These learning events are often supplemented by the offerings of external providers, as well as employee participation in traditional degree programs.

Given that the majority of these programs are paid for, or at least subsidized, by the organization, it is wise to pursue them to the fullest extent. Now that you have explored your career goals and potential, take the time to devise a formal development strategy that will help you reach your desired destination.

The Value of Trainers and Formal Training

I have a soft spot for teachers, trainers, and any individual who braves a classroom and actively makes a meaningful connection with program participants. For all the talk of informal development and commoditized e-learning, there really is no substitute for the classic "chalk and talk" model. However, my business side wishes it was as effective. After all, e-learning is cheaper, faster, more scalable, and easier to disseminate. But it's simply not as effective. Furthermore, while informal elements have merit as well, they are even harder to measure.

Classroom training has been and will remain a key element in supporting people's success, especially for those in functional roles and at pre-leader levels. You might not remember that statistics course now, but rest assured that it served a purpose. Just as the seemingly endless flight standard operating procedures served their purpose when I ran into that patch of trouble at five thousand feet.

But even required training doesn't have to be boring. Today's learning organizations demand that courses become more interactive – with assessments, simulations, and real-world role-plays that tie in with and support the other elements of effective learning. This presents two distinct opportunities for trainers. First, they can reshape the face time to make it even more memorable and impactful by teaching employees how to solve problems – even unforeseen ones – rather than simply recall facts. Second, they can ensure that the people who attend their courses become advocates for real-time learning back at the workplace.

The Challenge of Technology

If you are given the opportunity to attend a face-to-face training session, be it a formal college course or a company-sponsored event, try to be truly present. This means actively unplugging, a task that is especially difficult for those workers who believe that breath-mint-sized keyboards hold the path to enlightenment. I've yet to hear about the tweet that changed someone's life or the instant message that prompted a career change. You have to *experience* experiences. There is simply no shortcut.

Trainers are perfectly situated to impart successful habits that can truly enhance an employee's ability to perform. Trainers are the facilitators of experience, the ambassadors of coachable moments. Yes, in the cheaper, better, faster world of the "i_____" (insert appropriate Apple device), you have to bring your technological A game. In the end, however, e-learning is a hygiene factor – table stakes of a successful strategy. If you buy into the 70-20-10 model in its purest form, then classic face-to-face trainers are more important than ever.

To be successful in today's world, you have to make the most of your moments. This is especially true for job seekers and lifetime learners. Regardless of what is offered (or not) by your organization, you are the CEO of your own career. To be successful you must look for opportunities to learn in a variety of settings: formal classrooms, to be sure, but also on the job, in the moment and, most important, from the people with whom you interact.

Part 3: Taking Action

Congratulations! You've made it to the final stage of Phase 1.

By now you should have a clear understanding of your interests, skills, and values. You should also be well on your way to capitalizing on those qualities and propelling yourself to the next level.

Understanding Your Contribution Level

The following exercise will help determine your current contribution level – the value you provide and the impact you have in your current organization. Your responses will indicate whether you should look for more challenging opportunities within your current role or seek experiences in a different form or contribution level.

Self-Guided Exercise 8: Your Current Career Level

Read each statement in the various categories and decide whether or not it describes your work reality. If true, place an X in the box provided. Be sure your answers reflect the current reality of your situation and not what you wish it was or what your title conveys. If you currently manage staff, skip the first two contribution categories.

__Note:__ In some organizations, headcount (the number of people you manage) conveys power. In others, budget ownership, P&L contribution, or geographic influence provides an indication of importance. This is not to say that independent contributors are not vital to organizational success. There are several specialty roles that (while not having direct reports or responsibility for budget) carry significant weight and are viewed as critical simply due to the specialty of the role or skill set of the position holder. Regardless, it's important to be aware of your own situation and answer the questions below honestly.

Also, beware of the "title trap." A VP at a 100-person company may not carry the same weight as a Director in a 50,000-person global enterprise. It's important to understand the level at which you currently play and how potential employers may view it.

Dependent Contributor	
At this point in my career I ...	**True?**
1. Can handle the basics of my role, but need direction and additional guidance to tackle the more challenging deliverables.	
2. Keep my manager informed on the status of deliverables and any potential pitfalls or trouble spots.	
3. Ask thoughtful questions of my manager and colleagues, conduct research independently, and implement suggestions and lessons learned.	
4. Understand how my part fits into the whole, but spend the majority of time focusing on my responsibilities as outlined by my manager.	
5. Keep a pulse on customer needs and manager expectations, asking clarifying questions when needed.	

Independent Contributor	
At this point in my career I ...	**True?**
1. Have built a reputation as a strong team player who exercises good judgment.	
2. Can get to the root of most position-specific issues on my own and develop practical solutions without having to consult my manager.	
3. Assume responsibility for mastering position-critical skills and related technology.	
4. Develop creative solutions to conflicts or project-related challenges.	
5. Am I an effective project manager who can meet or exceed the expectations of my customers.	

Contribute Via Others*	
At this point in my career I ...	**True?**
1. Help newly hired direct reports seamlessly integrate to the organization.	
2. Use my organization-wide network to ensure my department and my direct reports are able to secure the information and support they need to complete projects.	
3. Act as a mentor to my direct reports as well as others within my reporting chain.	
4. Provide insightful coaching to team members, ensuring they learn and benefit from our discussions.	
5. Am trusted to lead projects with difficult deliverables and tight deadlines.	

* This does not assume or depend on a formal management title.

Note: In the past, the "contribute via others" category was reserved for line managers, i.e., those who have direct responsibility for employees via a traditional management structure. As companies become increasingly complex, matrix-oriented reporting chains and organization design structures are more common. This means that employees must work more collaboratively than ever before, operating as loose project teams. This reliance on core subject-matter expertise rather than traditional hierarchies can lead to employees holding multiple roles within the same job. For example, depending on your role, you could be a project leader one day (i.e., responsible for staff, budget, etc.), an ancillary team member the next, and a core expert the day after that. In fact, given the speed of business today, you may find yourself shifting roles multiple times in the same day as you move from project call to project call.

Take this reality into consideration as you complete this contribution level exercise. Revisit your answers as needed. The goal is to uncover the area in which you most often reside.

Intrepreneurial Contributor**	
At this point in my career I ...	**True?**
1. Exercise significant authority, influence, and impact over people, resources, and projects.	
2. Have the ability to quickly secure needed information from key stakeholders. Have the organizational clout to get face time with and shape the decisions of senior leaders.	
3. Influence important decisions and help shape the strategic direction of the organization.	
4. Have and can clearly communicate a compelling vision for my department and know how that ties into and supports the organization's vision and mission.	
5. Represent the organization to outside groups or customers.	

** Intrepreneurial refers to a corporate employee who develops new enterprises within the corporation. Remember that you can be an intrepreneurial contributor even if you are an independent contributor.

Quick Tip

Just as managers have different levels of experience, your employees may be at different stages of their careers and thus need different levels of guidance from you. If you are applying for a management position, be sure to keep these categories in mind. As you work through your career, you may find yourself managing dependent contributors – e.g., interns and seasoned intrepreneurs – at the same time. Clearly, to be effective you'll have to adjust your style and expectations to fit the situation.

Scoring

- If you answered "True" three or more times in a single contribution category, it is likely that you are currently functioning at that level.

- If you answered "True" three or more times in more than one category, it is likely that you have already begun the transitioning process. In many cases, the higher level is more representative of your reality.

Coach Exercise 4: Clarifying Your Contribution Level

Take a few moments to review your answers with your coach. Often, people feel pressure to place themselves in a "higher" category. If you are to advance, it's important to understand your current contribution level and how that supports or conflicts with your career goals.

Once you've affirmed your view, ask your coach how you can structure a productive conversation with your manager to validate your assumptions. It's painful when there is a clear disconnect between what you think you contribute and the value perceived for your services. Knowing the reality, however, is the only way to advance. Sometimes you may be pleasantly surprised by how your current actions are valued.

Align Your Goals with Company Objectives

It is not enough to want a new job or higher position. Furthermore, while taking accountability for gaining the required skills and experiences is a good first step, it doesn't guarantee success. There must be both a pressing organizational need for the services you hope to provide and a compelling case as to why *you* are the right person to provide them.

Remember that, in many cases, you are not just competing against other internal and external candidates for the role. Instead of increasing or replacing headcount, organizations can opt to fill the need through contractors or vendors, or can outsource the work to lower-cost countries. If you want to be hired, you have to demonstrate that your specific skills and abilities are uniquely positioned to fulfill their needs.

Note: This reality has become even more challenging in recent years for employees in the U.S. and Western Europe, as organizations wrestle with the unyielding pressure to deliver more for less. This often materializes as business-sponsored, HR-run "big data" analysis that takes aim at the Total Cost of Workforce (TCoW). The goal of these programs is to increase the financial health of an organization by shifting routine, transactional, delivery-oriented work to lower-cost countries and taking a more methodical approach to hiring. For example, instead of backfilling a position at the same grade level, managers are compelled to consider whether a more junior, lower-cost resource would suffice.

Nothing is wrong with these practices as long as they don't negatively impact quality of output, but they do present a new wrinkle for job seekers. In short, the world just got harder. Global business means global competition, so you have to be ready to be better than the other guy – even if the other guy is a world away. There are some jobs that are immune to realities of the global market – for example, you can't outsource a haircut. Thanks to advances in technology, however, these "safe positions" are few and far between. Given this reality, it's imperative you get your game face on.

One of the fastest ways to gain rapport with people is to have and draw attention to similar needs and interests. The same holds true for professional relationships, specifically hiring managers and the corporate needs they represent. If you can identify and acquire the skills your organization requires, and combine those skills with the indispensable quality of passion for your profession, you will ensure your success. The following exercise will provide an indication of where you stand in this regard.

Self-Guided Exercise 9: Goal Alignment

As you answer the questions, think of what you will need in terms of your desired position. Use the answers to assess your readiness for the role.

Company Needs: What is needed in the role?	
Question	**YES or NO**
1. Do you know and are you able to fulfill the needs of your primary internal and/or external customers?	
2. Do you have a process for seeking feedback from these customers regarding your performance?	
3. Can you explain how your daily work helps the strategic vision of the organization?	
4. Do you know what your new manager would expect from you?	
5. Do you understand what the organization expects from someone in that position and how those expectations will increase over time?	

Required Skills: What do you bring to the table?	
Question	**YES or NO**
1. Do you know the skills you must have to be effective in the job sought? Remember to think beyond the wish list presented in the job description. What is key to the role and the person to whom it reports?*****	
2. Do you have the technical skills required to contribute appropriately in the position sought?	
3. Do you have the "soft skills" (e.g., verbal/written communication, conceptual flexibility) required to excel in the position sought?	
4. Do you have a variety of skills and strengths that differentiate you from others who might also seek that job?	
5. Do you have the education, certifications, or formal training required to perform well if given the chance?	

*Quick Tip – Required Skills

One of the most impactful "return fire" interview questions I ever received from a candidate was: "If you hired me for the role, what is one thing that I could do to make your life easier?"

The question, which was obviously focused on a "win state" for me, the hiring manager, caused me to step back and actually think for a moment about what I would most value in a new direct report. I'd asked several candidates the "So, do you have any questions for me?" question that afternoon, and after hearing the same rehearsed, safe, standard replies this really stood out. We ended up extending the interview, during which I received more clarity about the person's ninety-day plan for success.

Don't forget that you're talking with a person – someone who has a myriad of work and home life responsibilities. Their job is to hire the best candidate and bring a win for the company in doing so. If you can truly connect and offer a personal win as well as an organizational win, you will be much better off.

Passions/Differentiators: What is your X factor?	
Question	**YES or NO**
1. Do you understand and appreciate the value of your chosen profession?	
2. Do you track and are you interested in the latest developments in your field?	
3. If money weren't an issue, would you still remain interested and involved in your chosen profession?	
4. Do you consistently think of ways to improve and/or make a mark on your profession?	
5. Can you think of a position that you would enjoy more?	

Scoring

For each question that you answered "Yes" assign yourself one point. Total the points according to the following equation:

Company Needs___ + Skills___ + Passions___ = Career Alignment

- If your total score is 12 or higher, you are in alignment.
- If your total score is between 9 and 11, you should make some changes to spice up your work life.
- If your total score is below 9, you need to rethink your current position and/or career.

Coach Exercise 5: Measuring the Gap

Discuss these finding and your options with your career coach. Take time to explore keys to driving greater alignment and/or consider alternatives.

Taking Action on the Five Success Factors

Success Factor 1: Improving Self Knowledge

No matter the status of your work/life situation, you have the ability to improve your circumstances. Throughout this assessment process you've uncovered areas to examine and enhance. But understanding and being able to convey your accomplishments is just as important. Being able to clearly communicate your successful past will help propel you to the greener pastures that are your future.

Track Your Accomplishments

Most people have a difficult time articulating their accomplishments ... if they can remember them at all. Interviews are hard enough. Tactfully navigating an informal work-related conversation with an influential contact or colleague can be even more trying, especially for my fellow introverts. To ensure you take full advantage of such opportunities, keep a running record of your career accomplishments.

Self-Guided Exercise 10: Noting Your Contribution

In the space below briefly describe a recent project of which you are particularly proud.

Quick Hint: *If you are struggling, ask yourself: What is the most important contribution I've made to the organization this year? Ideally, this should be something beyond your core job description.*

Your Contribution

_____

_____

_____

_____

_____

_____

_____

Once you develop a habit of committing your work-related successes to paper, begin organizing them into two logical groups: those that are **qualitative** in nature, e.g., speech-making and writing, and those that are **quantitative** in nature, e.g., project planning and budgeting. In both cases, think about the impact or, more specifically, the tangible return on investment (ROI) you produced.

Remember that even qualitatively oriented wins can have associated measures. For example, providing a series of training sessions on how to conduct performance reviews can impact associated scores on related employee engagement surveys. The trick is to be aware of the measures your company uses and what new measures you can build into your projects at the start of the process. As an organization development professional, I've learned that the impact of almost any endeavor can be measured if the project is thoughtfully designed.

Savvy career builders will take this a step further and begin to associate specific actions with each achievement. These are naturally framed via action verbs (*implemented*, *designed*, *crafted*, etc.) and set a positive tone for the description to follow. A detailed process for transforming these records into a workable, definitive resume can be found in Phase 2 of this book: "Building a Rock Star Resume."

Reaffirm Your Values

Before going further, take a close look at the accomplishment you described and, more important, consider the other accomplishments swimming about your brain. Are they consistent with your values? Is the hard work producing the desired result? Are you on track, or have you gotten off course and are now in the midst of chasing something you never really wanted?

Remember the first thing I said: "There is nothing more frustrating than succeeding in the wrong direction." Luckily, if you get off track your career coach can help you make a U-turn.

Success Factor 2: Partnering with Colleagues

Evaluate the Past

As an executive coach and certified 360 reviewer for multiple instruments, I'm often asked for "quick tips" or "how tos" for interpreting the feedback. Naturally it depends on the instrument involved, but there are some general guidelines to help you navigate the process.

- Ensure you understand the instrument and its associated report. If not provided automatically, request a debrief session from the provider or HR.
- Keep an open mind as you review the results.
- If you get tough or unexpected news, sleep on the results before reacting.
- Focus on trends rather than individual data points.
- Don't hyper-focus on the negative.
- Don't try to guess who said what. This is especially true if the 360 offers a verbatim section that shows screened comments from individual raters.
- Don't play investigator or stalk your raters. Simply thank them via a group email for their input.
- Respect confidentiality. Your manager is the only person whose scores will stand alone. You can and should request a debriefing session with him or her to discuss the results and development actions.
- You can ask follow-up questions of other raters, but only if you have a good relationship and the goal is greater understanding of trends – not an investigation of who said what.
- **Most important**, don't decrease the instrument's value before you begin by stacking the deck. In many cases, when used for development, participants will be allowed to select their own raters. If given the opportunity, select a representative pool of raters. This should include all direct reports (unless hired within the previous three months), your manager, and key customers, peers, and partners, regardless of your relationship. In others words, don't throw yourself a softball by having only your buddies rate you. First, given the confidentiality, they might not be as kind as you expect. Second, you could miss out on some key lessons. And finally, simply asking your "tough customers" for feedback often enhances the relationship.

Let's face it: for many, rereading past performance appraisals can seem as appealing as sifting through old tax returns in preparation for an audit. Still, the opinions and suggestions found in these documents can be vital career tools. Take the time to consider your old reviews, 360s, coaching conversations, and other bits of feedback received during the course of your career.

Self-Guided Exercise 11: Recalling Past Feedback

Use the space provided to make notes on what was said or written. Remember to focus on recurring themes and repetitive suggestions, as opposed to individual comments.

Past Feedback

_____

_____

_____

_____

_____

_____

_____

Now take a look at your notes and answer the following questions:

- *Do the trends and suggestions offered agree or conflict with your view?*
- *How have you changed or grown since your last review?*
- *How will this affect your next review? Commit to paper the actions you will take to make your next review better than the rest.*

Do you like the way you currently "show up" at work? What would you change if you could (and you can)? Take a minute to record your thoughts below.

Enhancing the Future

_____

_____

_____

_____

_____

_____

_____

Get a Second Opinion

Share the trends with your coach, trusted colleagues, and/or networking partners. Do they agree with your assessment and prior feedback? How have you grown during your time with them? What skills or abilities have you developed that make a difference in your work? What shortcomings persist despite your efforts to improve?

Once you have received their input on your current performance and their reactions to what was said about you in the past, you will begin to see a more accurate picture of your strengths, as well as the areas in which you need improvement.

Note: Keep an eye out for what people learned from you. The more you give, the more you get. Effective employees make a meaningful impact on the people with whom they come in contact. This is not an ego thing. It happens naturally, when you honestly care about seeing others succeed. This action, if authentic, pays dividends.

Success Factor 3: Becoming Organizationally Aware

The more you know about your organization, the better prepared you will be to capitalize on opportunities as they arise. While most people limit their research and understanding to their immediate team or department, the savvy career builder will work to attain a broader sense of the company and its inner workings.

The best way to get information is to give it first. Begin to make a name for yourself as someone who understands how his or her department affects the company. You'll be surprised by how quickly people come to you for information and how eager they are to explain their department and its goals to you.

Informational Interviews

A more proactive approach is to request informational interviews with key knowledge holders in other departments. These insightful discussions help you build networking relationships while affording you the opportunity to ask specific questions about other areas in the company.

While these interviews sometimes evolve into true dialogues, the majority provide a predominantly one-way flow of information. It is therefore critical that you respect the time of the person you are "interviewing." To ensure a successful discussion, arrive promptly, with clear and pertinent questions, and conclude at the scheduled time. Some helpful informational interview questions include:

- What initially attracted you to this profession?

- What were the surprises – good and bad?
- What does a typical day look like for you?
- What are the *must have* skills for this job?
- How has the profession changed during your tenure?
- What do you think the future of the profession will be?
- What's the best advice you never received (but wish you had) along the way?
- If given the opportunity, all things considered, would you make the same career choice?
- Is there anything I should have asked, but didn't?

Success Factor 4: Developing Your Options

The past is nothing in the face of the future.

Improving Today

One of the tools I use in my organization development work is called a **time signature study**. It's a detailed process that allows me to break apart any profession and compare excellence with adequacy. By systematically analyzing the difference between top performers and average performers through the lens of future needs, I'm able to design a position profile that's instrumental in managing the employee lifecycle for that role – everything from hiring and training to performance and talent management.

The work is invaluable to organizations as it increases the quality of hires and enhances the productivity and effectiveness of average-performing employees. The concepts involved in this sophisticated consultative work can be used by job seekers to gain clarity on the type of position he or she would like in the future. But it takes work.

Self-Guided Exercise 12: Your Personal Time Signature

There is nothing easy about pursuing career options. It takes energy. And you won't have energy if you are muddled in negativity due to your present circumstance. The best way to improve tomorrow is to improve today.

The chart below will help you analyze your current job by individual activity and provide some sense of how much of it currently meets your expectations.

Activity	Enjoy	Don't Enjoy	% of Time	Method of Increasing Fulfillment
Proposal writing		X	40%	Make more meaningful by seeing the bigger picture: • Learn financial software as a lead-in to pricing. • Request sales "ride along" to get a sense of customer interactions.

It is important that you increase your fulfillment by expanding those aspects of your position that you enjoy and minimizing those that cause you stress. While you certainly will not be able to delegate or avoid all "grunt work," this awareness will allow you to arrange your work pattern so the negative aspects are handled when you are in the proper frame of mind.

Building Tomorrow

Despite the road you have traveled in the past, the future holds a wealth of new possibilities. Consider all the options available to help you grow beyond your current situation.

Self-Guided Exercise 13: Exploring Options

In the space below list three attractive and attainable career development options that you can pursue right now. Remember that not all development options are reliant on upward job changes. Consider project assignments, lateral moves, or career changes.

Example: Applying for that open account-rep position will help me sharpen my influencing skills and will complement my industry and product knowledge. It could lead to a sales-management position in the future.

Career Development Options
1.
2.
3.

Now it's time to research these specific opportunities. If your focus is an extra project, contact your manager or the project leader for a description of the actual work involved, time requirements, and deadlines. If it is a job/career change, contact HR for a job description and appropriate internal contacts.

If you are looking externally, now is the time to nurture your network. In the next phase, "Building a Rock Star Resume," you will learn how to thoughtfully promote your accomplishments. Remember, once you reach out to a hiring manager or headhunter you have to be ready to submit a polished resume.

Success Factor 5: Making Career Plans

Choosing a Path

By now you should have a clear indication of the road you want to take. Now it's time to take a tough look at the reality of getting to your goal.

Self-Guided Exercise 14: Measuring Skill Gaps

In the space below, write your selected career goal. Once you've made your decision and are aware of the skill gaps holding you back, begin to pursue the necessary training to fill those areas.

Career Goal –			
Skill Required	**Have**	**Do Not Have**	**Plan for Development**

Walking the Path

Planning requires organization. Some people find organization in written notes, while others prefer a graphical representation of the facts. A matrix provides a combination.

Self-Guided Exercise 15: Cultivating Your Resources – Part 1

Design your career-plan matrix by doing the following:

- *List the departments for which you want to work.*
- *Identify networking contacts for each area. Be sure your partners are willing and able to provide information. Be ready to reciprocate.*
- *List the type of information you need.*

	Department 1	Department 2	Department 3	Department 4
Contacts				
Networking Partner*		X		X
Mentor**	X			
Information				
Skill Development				
Job Descriptions				
Openings				
People Profiles				
Recommendations				

*Networking Partners are typically able to provide insights to needs across multiple departments, or at least those outside your own view.

** **Mentors** most frequently help with guidance associated with their department or area of expertise.

Self-Guided Exercise 16: Cultivating Your Resources – Part 2

If you are seeking a role externally or are currently unemployed, use the following matrix to organize your next steps.

	Company 1	Company 2	Company 3	Company 4
Contacts				
Internal Contact*	X			
Headhunter**		X	X	X
Information				
Skill Development				
Job Descriptions				
Openings				
People Profiles				
Recommendations				

* **Internal Contacts** can serve as coaches for employment opportunities with their organization. Keep in mind that some companies offer employees referral fees for helping to secure tough placements. Make sure you understand the rules and follow the processes necessary to help your contacts secure their due rewards.

** **Headhunters/external recruiters** can be incredibly helpful in your job search, especially if you are in a specialized field and are mid- to senior level. They are typically secured by a company via a retained search and are paid a percentage-based fee for finding the right hire. Unlike other contacts, they have a clear monetary interest in helping you secure the position. That said, their success is dependent on the relationships they develop, so most endeavor to ensure that both sides of the equation see the placement as a long-term win.

The Final Step

The logical next step toward making your career dreams a reality is to commit what you've learned to paper in the most productive form – a working resume. The next phase, "Building a Rock Star Resume," will show you how.

During this time you also might want to have a meeting with your manager to discuss your findings and explore the opportunities for career growth. The following guidelines will help you outline and structure that important session.

Meeting with Your Manager

Now that you have a clear sense of where you are and where you wish to go, it is time to communicate this to the people who can help you get there. If you have a good relationship with your manager, the following guidelines will serve as a productive framework for your initial meeting. If not, use them to communicate with other influential people in your network. In either case, be sure to remember the following:

- Clearly communicate what you are hoping to achieve and why.
- Describe how your goals benefit the company and their department, if applicable.
- Respect their time and take their advice to heart by asking questions and actively listening.
- Share examples of your accomplishments, as appropriate.

Step One: Set Expectations

It is critical that you set a positive, productive tone early on. You should seem excited about your past experiences, yet eager to explore how you might contribute even more to the organization via your career goals. Make sure to cover/plan for the following:

- Have a clear purpose and agenda for the discussion. Don't be shy about sharing where you are in the job process, including your desired timeline for a potential move. For example, is this something you are just beginning to explore or do you have a specific internal job in mind?
- If unknown to your counterpart, briefly summarize your experiences and achievements in your current position. (Hopefully your manager does not have this problem.)

- If you've recently taken part in an assessment (e.g., a 360), share an overview of findings if the individual was involved.
- Communicate a desire to move beyond your present situation.
- Thank the person in advance for his or her willingness to help.

Step Two: Examine and Explore Possibilities

Unless you routinely engage in open communication with your manager, he or she may not even be aware that you long to grow your career. Help get him or her on the same page by quickly reviewing:

- The aspects of your work that you do and do not enjoy. (Be sure to do the latter tactfully.)
- Your understanding of your strengths and weaknesses.
- The areas of development you have uncovered and are working on.

Once you have presented your manager with this information, ask for feedback. Be sure to listen for both affirmations of your findings and areas where he or she has a different opinion. Next, ask for the following input regarding your primary career goal:

- How will exploring this opportunity affect me, you as my manager, and the company?
- What areas must I improve in to qualify?
- Is the career goal realistic in light of these factors?
- Will you support me?
- Be sensitive to his or her needs, i.e., ensure you have a replacement/succession plan in place for yourself if you are moving internally.

Step Three: Remove Barriers

Even if your manager acts as a career advocate for you, barriers may arise that could derail your plans. To ensure you are equipped to make the journey toward your goals, consider the following questions.

- What issues or responsibilities do you have outside of work that could affect your career plans?
- Are there internal players who would stand in your way? What are their motivations? Can they be swayed in your favor?

- Consider the timing – what deliverables do you have in your current role that could sideline plans for career advancement?

Note: When pressed, anyone can come up with a rationale for *not* pursuing his or her goals. As you ask yourself the questions above, it's important to note the difference between legitimate reasons (usually temporary and addressable) and excuses, which are often imaginary and thus lack an expiration date.

Step Four: Revise Your Thinking and Determine Next Steps

Sometimes you have to act as your own devil's advocate. Listing the many ways you could conceivably fail and/or actively attempting to talk yourself out of a goal can actually help strengthen your resolve and sharpen your plans for achieving that objective. So take the exercise above to heart, and then revise your plan of action.

Assuming your manager approves of your refined objective, you need to develop a time-sensitive plan for achieving it. Consider the following points as you discuss how to develop this plan:

- What support is available to help you bridge current skill gaps?
- Given your current workload, do you have the time to take needed training?
- How will other members of the department be affected by your actions?
- Will your manager act as a mentor for you?

Step Five: Commit to Metrics and Follow Up

Career plans are most effective when backed by managerial support and have specific dates for completing each action item. To achieve success, make sure you leave the meeting with the following:

- Clear support for your goal
- A broad outline of milestones related to the goal
- A date for the next planning meeting

Keep in mind that this is a high-view preliminary discussion. Chances are you will need to have several more conversations before you crystallize your plans. Be sure to take responsibility for scheduling these sessions and driving the discussions. Remember, it's your career.

But What If I Don't Have Managerial Support?

Sometimes your organization and/or manager will support your development goals. Sometimes they won't. Don't let a lack of formal support stop you from pursuing a meaningful development plan. The following steps can help you create an effective, personalized plan that will help you leverage your strengths or reduce your weaknesses.

Step 1: Analyze the Business Need

- Focus on the business – Note the major issues/objectives facing the organization, your business unit, and/or your team over the next six to twelve months.

Step 2: Examine Prior Feedback

- Focus on yourself – As you think about these priority issues, consider what you believe your contribution could or should be to their success. What impact you can have? Consider feedback you have received on your strengths and development areas.

Step 3: Select a Development Planning Approach

- **Option 1: Breadth Approach** – Use if you have two or three core competency strengths that need to be further leveraged and/or developed.
  - Select one of your priority business issues or projects and use that as your "vehicle for development."
  - Select **two or three** behaviors that you are going to develop.
  - Construct a plan for each behavior that relates to the key business driver.
- **Option 2: Depth Approach** – Use if you have a competency that is either a strong developmental need or so critical to your business issues that you feel you must focus on it alone.
  - Select the competency you wish to develop.
  - Select **two or three** priority business issues as "vehicles for development." Try to select very different situations.
  - Construct a plan that highlights how the competency can be demonstrated in each situation.

Step 4: Agree, Record, and Review

- If your manager is not supportive, take time to review the plan with a trusted colleague or your career coach. Then be sure to commit the plan to paper with clear milestones, like you would any other project. Throughout the year take time to review your progress.

Sample Breadth Approach	
Business Situation	**Relevant Competencies**
Lead a core team responsible for starting project ABC.	1. Interpersonal Understanding
	2. Impact and Influence
	3. Leadership
Interpersonal Understanding	**Measures**
Actions to Take	• Understand the 10 main issues and concerns of the team in relation to the project and have action plans to address each
• Conduct a confidential survey and run an open forum to ascertain the team's concerns, feelings, ideas, and suggestions regarding the project	• Team expresses that they feel their input is important to you
	• Conflict is surfaced and dealt with in a positive manner
Impact and Influence	**Measures**
Actions to Take	• Project is completed on time, within scope, and under budget, with no quality issues
• Conduct a series of presentations and/or Q&A sessions to keep stakeholders up to date so they can help the team achieve success	• Resourcing requirements list is developed and resources obtained
	• Team-member feedback is positive regarding support from the company
Leadership	**Measures**
Actions to Take	• Team has a charter, critical success factors, and measures of success
• Take responsibility for team development. Put in place systems and tools for team members to use that will help them develop the skills needed to complete the project	• Team has completed an exercise to uncover strengths and weaknesses and develop an action plan for roles and responsibilities
	• Team members share with you that they are happy with how the team has come together
	• By project end, someone from your team is ready to be a core team leader

Sample Depth Approach	
Competency Conceptual Flexibility	**Business Opportunities** 1. Business proposal to Company XYZ 2. Increase return on sales to exceed 10% 3. Sales team development
Business Opportunity 1 Actions to Take • Business proposal to Company XYZ that specifically identifies alternative ways of meeting the client's needs; compare the pros and cons of this with our existing ideas	**Measures** • At least three alternative approaches were identified before selecting best option for proposal submissions • Proposal is accepted by customer • Sales targets for Company XYZ are met • Client expresses appreciation for win-win solution
Business Opportunity 2 Actions to Take • Return on sales to exceed 10% by identifying several alternatives for increasing the metric and weighing pros and cons of each	**Measures** • 10+% return on sales • New incentive plan drives higher % return on sales • Salespeople satisfied with new incentive plan as measured by decreased turnover of high performers • Higher % of sales to more profitable customers
Business Opportunity 3 Actions to Take • Identify several options to achieve career development goals for your sales team for the year, weigh pros and cons	**Measures** • Exceed sales targets for the year by x% • Decreased turnover of high performers to x% • Sales team members openly discuss career goals with you • Your approach to development gets adopted by other parts of the organization

For additional samples of breath and depth development plans or details on how to roll out this process in your organization, please contact us at www.plotlineleadership.com.

Extra Credit – Your Brand Revisited

In Coaching Exercise 2 we asked that you describe your brand or personal value proposition (PVP). Specifically, we asked you to answer the following:

- What are you known for?
- If you were a product, how would a promoter describe you?

Coach Exercise 6: Your Brand – Take 2

Having come to the end of this phase, revisit your initial response and consider whether it still holds true. Take a few minutes to consider the following questions, and then discuss with your career coach.

- o Consider your initial description – is there anything you want to change?
- o What elements of your prior brand do you want to shed?
- o What do you want to be known for that people currently don't see (or is not there)?
- o How big is the gap between what others see and what you want to be known for?
- o Do you bring the right tools to the table or do you show up with seventeen spoons and a fish fork?
- o How can you leverage your existing strengths to produce better results en route to the next career opportunity?
- o Are your strengths and goals complementary or at odds?

Maintain your momentum. Review your accomplishments.
And get ready to formalize your thoughts via our next phase:

Building a Rock Star Resume.

Phase 2 – Building a Rock Star Resume

Purpose

A resume is more than a chronological listing of your job history. It's a complex marketing tool that, when well-crafted, can open the door to the interview process. This phase is designed to help you position yourself on paper in the best possible light.

Description

This phase will help you understand the marketing aspects of the resume and how to craft a professional document that will secure qualified interviews. Whether you're looking to change careers, apply for a new position, or simply change roles within your current organization, this section can help you reach your goal. Specifically, it will help you:

- Gain insight on how to craft a well-written cover letter
- Position yourself in the target job market
- Design an objective statement that clearly indicates the position desired
- Develop a professional summary that quickly highlights your accomplishments and increases your chances of getting the desired job
- Express achievements to maximize the likelihood of being viewed favorably by prospective employers
- Position your education, skills, publications, and volunteer activities appropriately to ensure maximum exposure

Introduction

Although everyone is unique, introverts and extroverts tend to have certain areas of strength and weakness when it comes to the job search process. Typically, introverts will be more apt to complete the self-assessment noted in Phase 1 and are generally more self-aware. Extroverts, given their largely external frame of reference, are typically better equipped for and have fewer reservations about the interview process explained in Phase 3.

Resume writing is the middle ground. Frankly, it's a tedious, rarely relished endeavor, but a critical component of the job search process. Regardless of your personality style, affinity for writing, or position on the introvert–extrovert scale, the tips and techniques presented in this phase will help you craft a rock star resume.

Interviews get you jobs.
Resumes get you interviews.

If you want a job you must convince the hiring manager and a series of other stakeholders that you are the right candidate for the position. Your resume is the key to earning that coveted face time.

While having the appropriate qualifications and experience naturally plays an important part in this undertaking, substance is only half the battle. The manner in which you present your career information is also critical. This phase will show you how to blend substance and style to create an intelligent, living document that grows with you as you move through your career.

A good resume results from a combination of thorough self-evaluation and skill analysis, as well as a detailed market survey that identifies specific job targets in the industries that interest you. Together, this information will help you position yourself strategically to hiring managers.

Often, however, you need a working resume to conduct the necessary research that clarifies the industries or fields you actually want to target. It's a bit of a chicken-and-egg paradox…but fear not! As your targets become clearer, you can revise your resume to create a better match between you and your goals. The initial draft just has to be workable enough to set you on the right path.

Resume Basics

The Purpose of Your Resume

A resume is more than a structured summary of one's employment history and qualifications. Today's resumes are thoughtfully crafted to highlight the impact you've made in other roles and, by association, what you can offer your next employer. They call attention to your professional strengths and downplay your weaknesses without distorting the facts or misrepresenting yourself. A good resume:

- **Is a marketing tool:** It leaves the reader with a positive impression of you after even a cursory review.
- **Sells you in your absence:** After you leave the interview, the decision-maker may want to discuss you with someone else. Your resume should help convince other stakeholders that you have a lot to offer.
- **Can guide the interview**: As the architect of the document, you have complete control over what the reader sees. If you highlight certain areas, the reader cannot help but ask about them. If you downplay or even omit other elements, you reduce the chances of having the interviewer center on those areas.

Please note: It is important to be truthful and accurate. Inflating titles and overstating results is never acceptable. That said, there are times when you might want to omit portions of your work history. Typically, this refers to items that are no longer relevant, e.g., the volunteer work you did while pursuing a master's degree.

When crafting your resume, it is important to emphasize:

- Things you have done well, enjoyed doing, and would like to do as part of your next position
- Areas that set you apart from other candidates
- Skills you possess that would be of interest to the hiring manager
- Experiences that are relevant to the job or company

Resume Myths and Facts

Everyone will have an opinion about your resume and the employment process. Be on the lookout for dated ideas and incorrect assumptions. The following myths and facts will help you avoid getting caught up in the paradigms of yesteryear.

Myths	Facts
• The purpose of a resume is to list all your skills and abilities.	• The purpose of a resume is to kindle an employer's interest and generate an interview.
• A good resume will get you the job you want.	• All a resume can do is get you in the door and give you the opportunity to have a conversation.
• An interested employer will read your resume carefully.	• Often your resume has less than thirty seconds to make an impression.
• The more good information you present in your resume, the better.	• Too much information may actually overwhelm and disinterest the reader.
• A resume should be one page.*	• If you have a thirty-year work history spanning five companies and two careers, you'd likely be hard pressed to shrink it to a page. Brevity is key, but take the space you need to tell your story.
• If you want a really good resume, have it prepared by a resume service.	• Many resume services use standard formats and processes that can appear generic. Although challenging, crafting a stellar resume is far from impossible. • Some headhunters (for high-end jobs) will help by providing high-level feedback, but the heavy lifting is always up to you. • If you elect to use a resume-writing service, be sure it offers a consultative interview that helps the writer truly understand who you are, what you've done, and where you want to go next. Also, be certain to obtain references and samples before engaging the vendor.

* Some professions, such as executive coach, speaker, trainer, or consultant, occasionally use a one-page professional bio. This tool, which should not be confused with a formal resume, is primarily used to provide potential clients or third-party booking agents with an overview of your background and offerings. The document

can afford to be shorter because interested parties either already have an understanding of your credentials and/or will seek additional information via your website. Those seeking full-time, part-time, or contract employment with a firm should focus on crafting a resume. If you are self-employed and would like information on designing a bio, log on to www.plotpointleadership.com. A copy of my bio is available on the site as an example.

General Resume Guidelines

While there are many schools of thought regarding resumes, there are a number of truisms that have stood the test of time. When preparing your document, consider the following:

- Restate your background in terms your target market will understand. Do not use the jargon of your present industry or company. For example, if you want to switch from education to a training position in the corporate world, remember that companies may favor "course" or "program" developers as opposed to "curriculum" developers. They are the same thing, really – just different slants on the end product.

- Most people need only one resume. However, if you have a diverse or specialized skill set you may want to write several versions of your resume to suit the different potential roles. On occasion, headhunters will have you rewrite your resume to meet the specific expectations and preferences of a potential employer.
    - o For example, an HR professional who has worked as a strategic business partner and in both leadership development and compensation may seek to emphasize the breadth of his experience when applying for a generalist role and the depth of work in a single area when applying for a position in a specific subspecialty. In both cases the facts should be correct, but what you highlight can make a real difference.

- Always have a professional summary on your resume. It is a powerful tool that dramatically influences the way the reader sees you and is the lens through which they view the rest of the information you have included.

- Omit personal details that are irrelevant to the job you are seeking, as these could be viewed as negatives or unintentionally used to discriminate against you.

- List job-related volunteer activities, especially those that highlight your professional strengths or other qualities and competencies that align to the position you seek.

Common Resume Problems and How to Avoid Them

Never be so eager to obtain a position that you sacrifice your integrity. Avoid the following at all costs:

- **Dishonesty**: Make sure you truly have the experience and expertise that you claim. Also, be sure to avoid boastfulness in your writing style. Remember, any claim made on the resume can be explored during the interview. For example, did you really "manage China," or did you provide marketing support to your five-person team in Shanghai?

- **Improper Length**: Forget the one-page rule. Your resume should be long enough to highlight your background and most relevant experiences. Research and follow the common practices in your chosen profession. For example, professors in a traditional academic setting and scientific researchers typically list all their publications. This section alone can far exceed the length of resumes in other professions. Also, as noted above, you have to consider the duration of you career. While no hiring manager wants to shuffle through a ten-page document, alarm bells will go off if you are able to fit a forty-year career onto a single sheet.

- **Hard to Read**: Go easy on the reader's eyes. Make sure you have enough "white space," indents, and boldfacing for visual interest. Also, use standard fonts like twelve-point Arial or Times, with one-inch margins. And forget about colored paper. Most resumes are emailed, so the extra expense is not worth it.

- **Wordy**: Keep descriptions brief and to the point, using simple, accurate language.

- **Too Slick**: Avoid flowery descriptors, as this could raise questions about whether or not the qualifications have been exaggerated. Every industry has jargon, and knowing the code can be helpful. Just make sure your words *mean* something. Writing something like "the big picture impact of reducing silos in an effort to enhance departmental synergy and create more bandwidth so we can better leverage our customer-focused client portfolio" might sound impressive to the novice reader, but it communicates next to nothing. Use real language and focus on the actual results achieved, quantifying where possible.

- **Amateurish**: Be sure you show an understanding of the business world, or of a particular industry or sector, by including the right information and presenting it professionally. Don't refer to the irrelevant or the dated.

- **Errors**. Carefully proofread your resume for spelling, punctuation, and grammar, and also give it to a skilled proofreader to check over. An error-free resume tells the interviewer that you have good communication skills and an eye for detail.

Part 1: The Cover Letter

A good cover letter introduces you to the potential employer. It conveys your interest in both the organization and the specific position, while at the same time briefly noting why you would be the right choice. A cover letter also introduces and supports the enclosed/attached resume. It is a perfect medium for highlighting additional skills or experiences that may not be noted on your resume.

Parts of a Cover Letter

The First Paragraph

Relationships are a key factor in all of life's endeavors, but they are of critical importance when you're looking for a new position. Anything you can do to capitalize on a relationship and build rapport with the reader will increase your chances of having your resume thoroughly reviewed. Therefore, it is imperative that you reference the relationship you have with the potential employer in the first paragraph.

In some cases your relationship with the reader and/or ultimate decision maker will be clearly defined (e.g., your brother knows him or her). In other cases, the relationship will not result from a personal association, but rather through a medium such as a corporate posting, third-party listing, or LinkedIn connection.

There are four types of interactions through which relationships are born. You must be able to craft opening paragraphs that are sensitive to each situation. The types of relationships are ranked below in order of effectiveness:

- **Direct**: You know or have recently met the person
- **Indirect**: You have been referred to the person by a direct contact
- **Responsive**: You obtained the lead via a corporate posting or third-party listing
- **Cold**: You are simply approaching companies (more specifically, their staffing departments) that may have opportunities

Examples:

- **Direct**: John, It was great to see you again at conference ABC. Thank you for alerting me to the open administrative assistant position at your organization.
- **Indirect**: Mr. Smith, Thank you for taking the time to speak with me regarding your vacant administrative assistant position. I'll pass on your regards to our

mutual colleague XXX. As I mentioned, I have five years of experience in that field and am eager to continue my career at Company X.

- **Responsive**: Mr. Smith, I recently read your job posting on Monster.com seeking an experienced administrative assistant. I am a dedicated professional with over five years of experience in that field and am eager to continue my career at Company X.
- **Cold**: Mr. Smith, I am writing to inquire whether you have any openings for administrative assistants. I am a dedicated professional with over five years of experience in that field and am eager to continue my career at Company X.

A Word on LinkedIn

Since its launch in 2003, LinkedIn has played an increasingly important role in the job search process. We'll discuss the service in greater detail toward the end of this phase, but the topic deserves a mention as we discuss types of connections.

Searching for a job, especially when you are out of work, can be a stressful endeavor. And while the pressure to connect is great, avoid committing a networking faux pas by mindlessly clicking the *connect* button on LinkedIn. People understand the desire to build connections, but they should be based on an actual interaction.

Take time to review the person's profile before sending the invitation. If you know them (and you should), personalize the invitation to note the connection. On the rare occasions when you *connect* before having met (at least virtually), take the time to clarify the reason for your interest. Ideally, you could send an *InMail* that explains your interest in connecting, e.g., obtain more detail about a job posting, and then follow up with an invitation.

This is one area where you should follow the proverbial grandma's etiquette advice. Doing so can be the difference between coming across as professional and coming across as desperate. Desperate is never attractive.

The Second Paragraph

The second and (if necessary) third paragraphs briefly highlight your skills and experiences, while at the same time conveying actual interest in obtaining the position.

Example: Career Transition (corporate to academia)

My corporate experience allowed me to gather and develop a wealth of transferable skills for use in the teaching profession, including people management, project planning, and creative team-based problem solving. I currently hold a BS in Psychology from Iona College and am working toward an MS in Elementary Education at Pace University. Pertinent, completed coursework includes: Personality Psychology, Teaching and Learning, Foundations of Education, Learning and Development, and Science Methods-Interdisciplinary Teaching N-6.

Joining the staff of School XYZ would be a great opportunity for me to fulfill my goal of working with children while making an impact on their learning and development. As a lifelong resident of XXX and former student in the school district, I have a keen understanding of the community and the many cultures and competency levels of its residents.

Example: Human Resources Professional

Over the past ten years I've demonstrated the ability to effectively manage processes, projects, and people for both small companies and large organizations. To further differentiate myself from other experienced MBAs I offer the following points of distinction:

- Published writer
- Presentation experience
- Deadline driven

- International experience
- Effective teacher/trainer
- Proven leader

In addition to the skills and abilities noted in your job description, I would bring to the table a wealth of practical business experience and a distinct passion for the training and development industry.

The Third Paragraph

The third and final paragraph lets the reader know that you have attached/enclosed a resume. More important, it makes a call for action and expresses the manner in which you will follow up.

Example: Career Transition (corporate to academia)

I've enclosed/attached a copy of my resume, which details my professional experience and educational credentials. I am available for employment immediately and would appreciate the opportunity to meet with you regarding potential opportunities. I will follow up with you once you have had an opportunity to review this information. Thank you for your time and consideration.

Example: Human Resources Professional

I have thoroughly reviewed your organization's website and feel I would make a welcome addition to your team. To that end, I've attached/enclosed a copy of my resume for your review. I will contact you by phone next week with an eye toward scheduling an interview. I look forward to speaking with you.

Craft Your Cover Letter

Self-Guided Exercise 17: Your Draft Cover Letter

Using the examples above as a guide, take a few moments to create a draft cover letter. Get the most out of the exercise by tailoring the letter for a specific opportunity you are reviewing now.

The First Paragraph

_____

_____

_____

_____

_____

_____

_____

The Second Paragraph

_____

_____

_____

_____

_____

_____

The Third Paragraph

_____

_____

_____

_____

_____

Importance of the Cover Letter

Be honest. Did you just blow past that section without drafting a cover letter? I'm not surprised if you did. Given the proliferation of online job-search mediums, the cover letter has largely fallen out of favor, replaced by contact forms and auto fillers.

Still, there is something to be said for heeding your grandmother's advice and leveraging the power of etiquette. While not a must have, a well-written cover letter that introduces and complements the details presented in your resume can help you stand out. Anyone can click a button, spamming potential employers with paperwork. Taking the time to write a targeted letter to a specific employer about a specific job demonstrates sincere interest. It may not win you the role, but in a tight market every advantage counts.

Sample Cover Letter

Peter Parker
738 Winter Garden Drive
Forest Hills, Queens, NY 10801

Date

Daily Bugle
10 39th Street
New York, NY 10801

Mr. Jameson,

Thank you for taking the time to speak with me regarding your vacant photojournalist position. As I mentioned, I have five years of experience as a freelance photographer and am eager to continue my career at your organization.

During my career I've demonstrated the ability to effectively capture quality images for newspapers, magazines, and specialized print publications. To further differentiate myself from other experienced professionals I offer the following points of distinction:

- Published writer
- Deadline driven
- Web minded
- Effective graphic artist

I have attached a copy of my resume, which further details my education and professional credentials. If your organization has room for a flexible professional with a proven track record for obtaining creative imagery, I would be interested in discussing employment opportunities. Thank you for your consideration.

Kind regards,

Peter Parker

Part 2: Defining Your Perfect Position

Job targeting is a process in which you consider your professional goals and abilities, and then uncover the specific opportunities that will best complement them. The more honest you are during this reflection, the better your chances are of making a match.

Understanding What You Really Want

As I noted in Phase 1, there is nothing more frustrating than succeeding in the wrong direction. To ensure that you are chasing the right job, ask yourself the following:

- What would be an ideal day at work?
- Which type of work do I really enjoy?
- What parts of my current/prior job(s) would I like to leave behind?
- How much do I want to earn?
- How far do I want to advance?
- What type of industry and organization do I want to work for?
- What type of organizational culture suits me best?

Self-Guided Exercise 18: Dream Job

Review the answer you provided in Self-Guided Exercise 7. Having completed the self-assessment, this is your chance to get even more specific. Take the time to picture your perfect profession. While we all can't be professional athletes, astronauts, or actors, it doesn't mean that your dream job is out of reach. Identify roles that contain those elements and really explore them.

As you think of your perfect day, describe everything, from what you would do to the office you'd have (if you had one), to the kind of clothes you would wear each day. Write it in the space below:

Dream Job

_____

_____

_____

_____

_____

And now, just for fun, ask yourself: "What would I want to do if money was not an issue?" Write your answer in the space provided.

_____

_____

_____

_____

_____

Understanding What You Have to Offer

People often use the phrase "He/She's one in a million" when describing someone who is exceptionally talented or stands above the rest of the field in a particular endeavor. The trouble is, in the reality of global competition, even when you are "one in a million" there are 7,200 people just like you. Think of this concept in terms of your chosen profession. If you are to succeed, you'll need to deliver an "X factor" that helps distinguish you from the competition.

In life you have to give to get. If you intend to secure the type of position you just described you must be prepared to offer the employer more than the rest of the flock. Having a clear picture of your value will not only help sell yourself, it can also isolate specific skills that need further development. Ask yourself:

- What work experiences have I obtained?

- What special skills set me apart?

- What education and training have I undergone?

- Do I have a personality that attracts people and brings out their best?

- Do I consistently give 100%?

- Do I take calculated risks and either succeed or learn from my mistakes?

Self-Guided Exercise 19: Elevator Speech

Take a moment to describe, in general terms, what sets you apart from other candidates. Think of it as a ninety-second commercial about yourself. (This will eventually become your Professional Summary.)

Your Elevator Speech

_____

_____

_____

_____

_____

Would you hire the person described above? Why? If not, what's missing?

_____

_____

_____

_____

Now that you have a feel for what you want and where you stand, let's uncover and position your actual accomplishments and experiences.

Part 3: Discovering Your Accomplishments

Focusing on Accomplishments and Achievements

Often people focus on describing past jobs instead of highlighting the accomplishments and achievements they made in those positions. Unfortunately, the resume screener and, later, the hiring manager are more interested in what you actually did than the titles you held.

Remember, titles mean different things in different organizations. And while the size and scale of the company can provide clues as to the actual scope of your role, other factors such as industry play a part as well. For example, a Vice President title, while impressive in some industries, is quite common in banking. Also, your profession can influence the terms used. Consultants and lawyers chase Partner, not Director. Within sales organizations, internal titles vary and often take backseats to external references designed to align "like for like" with customers. The point is simple – a fancy title is meaningless if you fail to document your accomplishments in the role.

In addition, most job hunters tend to ignore the accomplishments they made early in their careers. However, these are worth communicating because they let the reader know that you have a **history of achievement**.

Depending on how many jobs you have held, this part of your resume may be as long as a page or as short as a paragraph. The fewer jobs you list, the more accomplishments you should try to uncover. The more jobs you list, the more selective you can be about the accomplishments you include. Seasoned job seekers will create a database of accomplishments that can be searched and highlighted for inclusion on tailored resumes. These examples can also be used as talking points during the interview process.

This can be especially valuable for introverts, who typically prefer to internally process questions (think before speaking), as opposed to extroverts, who often verbally process (talk through their thoughts). The following exercises will help you prepare for detailed interview conversations. Having poignant examples of key skills and experiences will reduce the need to think on the fly, while still allowing you to add additional detail about the topics so as not to appear rehearsed.

Extroverts can also benefit from this exercise (and the ones to follow), as the upfront preparation will help ensure that you don't come across as if you are simply "winging it" – a huge turn off for some interviewers, especially introverts.

Skill Evaluation

Before setting out to write your resume, you should take the time to review your achievements and take stock of your current skills and abilities. This inventory will not only highlight attributes to be communicated to the potential employers; it will also help you identify career-related weakness. Both points of knowledge, when acted upon, can translate into a better position at a higher salary. To begin the personal skill-analysis process, complete the following exercise.

Self-Guided Exercise 20: Skill Evaluation

Exercise: Examine your current resume and reflect on the experiences you've obtained thus far in your career. For each position, both paid and volunteer, place a check next to the skill used. If you've used the skill more than once, place several checkmarks. The goal is to determine a skill pattern – highlighting what you now know and drawing attention to skills you've yet to develop.

Note: The skills are listed as action verbs. These verbs will later be incorporated into the final resume as a way of highlighting your abilities. I'll refer to these skills as Success Factors.

As you complete the exercise think of these descriptors in terms of both qualitative and quantitative achievements. For example, did you analyze your company's proposal process find and remedy gaps, increasing efficiency by 10 percent? Did you author a new policy document that clarified a key procedure? Feel free to add others as you work with your career coach.

Skill	1	2	3	4	5	6	7	8	9	10	Total
Administered											
Analyzed											
Authored											
Budgeted											
Built											
Coached											

Skill	1	2	3	4	5	6	7	8	9	10	Total
Compiled											
Conceived											
Converted											
Coordinated											
Counseled											
Crafted											
Created											
Demonstrated											
Designed											
Developed											
Directed											
Established procedure											
Evaluated											
Hired											
Implemented											
Improved											
Increased											
Initiated											
Innovated											
Invented											
Liaised											
Presented											
Managed people											
Managed projects											

Skill	1	2	3	4	5	6	7	8	9	10	Total
Managed inventory											
Marketed											
Negotiated											
Networked											
Observed											
Organized											
Persuaded											
Planned											
Problem-solved											
Programmed											
Projected											
Purchased											
Reengineered											
Recommended											
Relocated											
Reorganized											
Researched											
Sold											
Supervised											
Taught											
Trained											
Troubleshot											
Upgraded											

Accomplishment Analysis

Now that you've reviewed the skills/success factors you've accumulated thus far in your career, take a few moments to highlight the most prevalent and important ones.

Note: You may also check items that you have a strong interest in. However, be aware that if you would like to incorporate these elements into your next position, you must have a concrete plan for acquiring the needed experiences and skills.

> ### *Self-Guided Exercise 21: Accomplishment Analysis*
>
> *Following the instructions below, isolate your qualitative and quantitative skills in preparation for further review.*

Step 1: Isolate Skill Categories

- Examine the previous exercise and note the most prevalent descriptors for each of your accomplishments.
- Select and list six quantitative and six qualitative descriptors. Having a combination (at least two from each category) will make you appear well rounded and therefore more salable to potential employers.

Note: Quantitative Accomplishments involve numbers and functional skills, while Qualitative Accomplishments deal with "softer" abilities such as managing and selling. Remember, however, that this exercise is somewhat subjective. For example, a traditional qualitative skill such as teaching could harbor quantitative attributes depending on the subject matter (e.g., science or math). It can also be affected by the strategic intent of your work – for example, the teaching you provided helped improve reading scores by 10 percent. How you define and categorize each accomplishment will provide you and your coach with insight on how you view your current skill sets.

Quantitative Accomplishments	Qualitative Accomplishments
1.	1.
2.	2.
3.	3.
4.	4.
5.	5.
6.	6.

Step 2: Prune and Prioritize Your List

Pick your eight strongest skills from the list above and write them in the chart below. These are your Personal Success Factors.

Most Prevalent Success Factors	
1.	5.
2.	6.
3.	7.
4.	8.

Accomplishment Validation

The next step in this process is to validate your accomplishments with specific examples of achievement from your work experience. These professional wins will not only lay the groundwork for your resume, they will also guide your interaction in the interview.

Step 1: Crafting Your "CAR" Stories

Isolating what **you really did** and crafting it into a well-written CAR statement (Challenging Situation, Action, and Result) is much more difficult than simply reciting your job description.

People, especially those who are highly accomplished, often struggle to express what they have done. This is partly a memory issue, but it also has to do with the pace of change and the demands placed on today's workers. Often professionals are so busy producing results they rarely have time to take stock of and learn from prior efforts before jumping into the next task or project. In other cases, it's a question of humility (a great thing, mind you!). Some people have a hard time giving themselves credit for the work produced. Don't get me wrong, "we language" has its place, but it can also muddle the context of your pitch. You have to be clear about what *you* did and how that affected the work.

When you write your CARs, consult the past for material, but also think about your future and the parts of your accomplishments you may want to emphasize as you pursue the next role.

Be sure to consider the problems and challenges you have faced in the job. How did you handle them? What was the result for your company? Remember, the ability to turn a negative into a positive, problem solving, and creative conflict management are highly sought-after skills.

Self-Guided Exercise 22: Draft CAR Stories

Write a CAR story for three of the eight success factors you listed.

Remember, the purpose is to get you to express your achievements in a succinct way. Therefore each CAR story should be forty words or less, organized in three sentences. These sentences present the:

- **Challenging Situation:** What was the problem or challenge you faced?
- **Action You Took:** How did you overcome it?
- **Results You Achieved:** What were the quantitative and/or qualitative results for the organization? When you can, use actual dollars and percentages to help illustrate and support your claims.

For example:

Success Factor: Increased Sales

- **Challenging Situation:** Company's products needed a fresh image to increase sales.
- **Action You Took:** Developed a new logo and branding strategy to appeal to a broader global market.
- **Result You Achieved:** Gave a new look to our products and increased sales by 18 percent.

Now you try one!

Success Factor: _____
Challenging Situation:
Action:
Result:

Getting stuck? No problem! Take a moment to refresh your memory and recharge your creative energies. The following prompting questions will help you recall your successes. In addition, sample stories appear at the end of this section.

Prompting Questions

Some people have a hard time recalling their accomplishments. Chances are, you have done more than you give yourself credit for. To help spur your memory, try asking yourself the following. Did you:

1. Help increase sales or market share?
2. Save the company money or contain costs?
3. Develop new business, enlarge a market, or increase the client base?
4. Help implement a new procedure or system?
5. Roll out a new product or program?
6. Successfully handle an emergency situation?
7. Identify and satisfy a need?
8. Make an active contribution to any company change?

9. Demonstrate leadership in the face of a challenge?
10. Solve a major or recurring problem for your department?
11. Do anything for the first time at your company?
12. Make a job easier or more efficient?
13. Improve quality?
14. Train anyone?
15. Voluntarily assume responsibility for a special project?
16. Reduce errors?
17. Exceed your goals or objectives?
18. Achieve equal results with fewer resources?
19. Manage other employees?
20. Improve employee performance?
21. Substitute for the manager in his/her absence?
22. Write anything for the company?
23. Make a presentation at an industry conference or event?
24. Volunteer for special committees, groups, or task forces?
25. Receive any awards?
26. Dazzle a customer with a new insight or excellent service?

You can also consider the following:

27. Your Brand: Are you known for handling certain types of difficult problems, situations, or people?
28. Your Performance: Did your exceed expectations on a recent performance or project review?

Now take a few minutes to complete the exercise.

Success Factor: _____

Challenging Situation:

Action:

Result:

Success Factor: _____

Challenging Situation:

Action:

Result:

Step 2: Rewriting Your CAR Statements

Now rewrite your CAR statements, further condensing the story into a two- or three-sentence description. These will appear as bulleted highlights under the general job description in the professional experience section of your resume. They illustrate how you exceeded the requirements of each position held.

Success Factor: _____
CAR Statement 1:
Success Factor: _____
CAR Statement 2:
Success Factor: _____
CAR Statement 3:

Sample CAR Statements

Success Component: Increased Business

Increased health and wellness plan participation from 350 to 600 enrollees by translating supporting documents into Japanese and establishing clear lines of communication to answer participants' questions. Improved client relations and increased profits by 10%.

Success Component: Implemented

Implemented a $10 million project installing backup servers. Completed installation on time, under budget, and with no unscheduled downtime. The project enhanced the risk coverage and responsiveness for the organization and its customers.

Success Component: Established

As cofounder of NE Martial Arts Academy, I was involved in fundraising, securing staff, program development, and tournament promotion. During its first year of operation, the nonprofit organization brought martial arts programs to 300 grade-school children in five communities and hosted two goodwill tournaments.

Success Component: Relocated

Relocated $120 million Regional Sales Office into new quarters. Negotiated rates and schedules, designed interior space, plan, and furnishings, and supervised construction of 10,000-square-foot addition. Move was accomplished without interruption of service to the business or sales force.

Success Component: Reorganized

After stepping in as the new manager, I reorganized staff goals to address a 30% turnover rate in the HR department. Through goal-setting and needs-assessment meetings, employees were able to voice opinions and reestablish expectation levels. Turnover was reduced by 10% in one year.

Additional Examples – Job Specific

The following examples illustrate how the bulleted CAR statements support the basic job description while highlighting the achievements you most want to convey to your potential employer. As you can see, CAR statements can be as simple as a brief note regarding the accomplishment, or can be quite detailed when describing complex projects.

Adjunct Professor

Designed and instructed a variety of courses in U.S. History. Wrote exams, organized assignments according to school specifications, and developed special projects to facilitate learning. Counseled students regarding their educational needs. **Key accomplishments** [Note: these are your CAR statements] include:

- Led a multidisciplinary team in the restructuring and redevelopment of the college's capstone course. Increased placement rate by 12%.
- Earned a Presidential Commendation for course design and student satisfaction. Efforts helped increase retention by 5%.

IT Representative

As lead of a Data Warehouse project team I was responsible for submitting, monitoring, tracking, and troubleshooting production. Provided support for the mainframe "Data Acquisition" processes: Key accomplishments include:

- Redesigned six major processes by creating Data Flow Diagrams and publishing technical specifications for super-users. Project completed on time and under budget.
- Conducted user meetings to analyze system requirements, modified existing programs, wrote new programs to handle gaps in performance, and oversaw the implementation of the updated system. Project increased user efficiency by 15%.
- Streamlined the individual processes, created Data and Process Flow Diagrams, and coordinated the scheduling of the "data acquisition" jobs with the client's technical staff. Efforts increased worker productivity while boosting morale.

Organizational Development Director

Performed a variety of activities, including scorecard development, culture-change programs, senior leader on-boardings, 360 feedback instruments, personality assessments, leadership development programs, team chartering, and meeting facilitation. Key accomplishments include:

- Facilitated a cross-functional project aimed at revitalizing the global sales force and designing a **customer-focused sales culture**. Conducted global data gathering and needs analysis, identified and assimilated internal and industry best practices, and developed a toolkit for sales professionals. Obtained leadership buy-in, developed metrics for implementation, and facilitated action planning sessions with sales and marketing teams.
- Led a cross-functional, international team to implement an award-winning global **Performance Management System**. The project, which was completed ahead of schedule and under budget, sparked an 18% improvement in employee engagement scores.

- Designed a global process for **courseware administration and delivery**. Used a blend of internal and external resources to increase efficiency by 25% and reduce costs by 20%.

Note: CAR statements are your key selling points, your differentiators: the things that will make you stand out from your competition. They will also whet the appetite of the reader, so he or she will want to meet you. Remember, the purpose of a resume and cover letter is not to archive your every action, but to get interviews. During the interview, you can elaborate on your experiences.

Always bring a copy of your resume to the interview.
CAR statements are excellent talking points and serve as quick reminders of your accomplishments.

Part 4: Parts of the Resume

Objective Statements

Once a virtual requirement of the resume, objective statements have largely fallen out of favor in recent years, especially with those seeking mid- to high-level positions. Still, the objective does have a purpose and can help job seekers at the beginning of their careers and those looking for a specific position.

Typically an objective statement begins with the words "To obtain" and goes on to describe, in one sentence, exactly the type of position the person is seeking. It sounds simple enough, but be wary of making sweeping generalizations or using clichés that tell the employer nothing and fail to distinguish you from the fray. Here's an example of a poor objective statement: "To obtain a challenging job working with people in a secure company that will utilize all of my abilities."

Instead, hone in on exactly what you want: "To obtain an administrative assistant position in the human resources department of an international marketing firm where I can use my expertise in the Microsoft Office Suite."

Note: There is a danger of pigeonholing yourself, but this can be alleviated by consistently changing your objective to mirror the needs of the employer and the individual job posting.

Professional Summaries

To find the job you want you must position yourself. This means stating your skills, experiences, competencies, and characteristics in a way that makes it easy for the prospective employer to see you in the open role or in other positions down the road.

To properly position yourself, you will need to develop a professional summary that sells, bringing together your accomplishments while allowing you to emphasize certain parts of your background and deemphasize others.

Designing a professional summary is not easy, but it is worth the time. A well-crafted summary can focus your job search and clarify the information you provide both before and during the interview.

Note: The rest of your resume should support the professional summary. For example, if the summary says that you are a financial wizard, the resume should offer significant proof of that claim.

Consider Your Audience

You may want to stay in your present company. In that case, you should position yourself to the person in charge of hiring for the particular department you want to enter. In other cases, you may want to go to a new company or even a new industry. In those instances, you should position yourself to a new employer. Either way, the steps are the same:

1. Decide what skills and qualities your prospective employer wants
2. Search your background to see where you have demonstrated complementary results
3. Write a summary and use it as the basis for your resume
4. Use the summary to sell yourself during an interview

Examples:

Researcher

An experienced researcher, analyst, and technical writer with a proven ability to grasp new information and concepts quickly. A seasoned public speaker with the ability to exceed client expectations. A dedicated project manager and problem solver with advanced computer skills. Excellent communicator, with foreign language abilities in Spanish, Portuguese, and Italian.

Marketing Manager

An experienced marketing professional with an affinity for developing high-performing sales support teams. A strategic thinker with the ability to leverage relevant IT tools and systems. A powerful proactive communicator. An experienced project manager with the ability to meet and exceed the expectations of internal and external clients.

Project Manager

A certified PM with over fifteen years of experience in successfully managing complex global projects. Solid experience in setting and maintaining project schedules and budgets, prioritizing workloads, and maximizing performance of project teams to complete projects cost-effectively and on time. Strong persuasive and motivational skills.

Programmer

A deadline-driven programmer with the ability to meet and exceed the needs of internal and external clients. A dedicated, people-minded project manager and problem solver. An excellent communicator with the ability to author, develop, and implement new programs. Key technical qualifications include: [Insert applicable operating systems, computer languages, programs, testing tools, etc.]

Self-Guided Exercise 23: Draft Professional Summary

Write your own summary statement in the space below.

Draft Professional Summary

_____

_____

_____

_____

_____

_____

Professional Experience Section

This is the portion of your resume where you list the general responsibilities and accountabilities you had in each of the positions you held during your career. This forms the backbone of your resume, noting what you've done and where you gained that experience. The basic description should be short and factual, and should highlight those tasks that you would like to perform in your next position.

Remember to start with your most recent position. State your title, company name, and employment dates, and then list your responsibilities. However, rather than ranking them chronologically, list them in the order of interest to the reader. Then follow the same procedure for your other jobs.

Example

Company X: Somewhere, NY – 2013–Present
Junior Trainer

Responsible for developing and instructing orientation and communication courses. Given primary coaching responsibility for incoming employees. Served on human resources and retention planning committees. Key accomplishments include:

- *This is where you list your applicable CAR statements.*

Note: The bulleted CAR statements explained in the last section follow this basic description. Again, these statements demonstrate how you rose above the general tasks required of your job.

Spice Up Your Language

In addition to the action verbs noted in the CAR statement section, try to jazz up the wording of your basic responsibilities. The following word choices should get you started, but consider working with your coach to explore other groupings that better align with your chosen profession.

Competence	
• Qualified	• Certified
• Adept at	• Aptitude for
• Experienced	• Practical approach to
• Performance-oriented	• Proven track record

Detail-Oriented	
• Accurate	• Analytical
• Deadline-driven	• Precise
• Methodical	• Careful
• Systematic	• Organized
Leadership	
• Headed/Led	• Developed subordinates
• Directed	• Coach
• Decision-maker	• Project/People-minded

Education

It is also important to list your educational credentials on the resume. Typically this consists of the school attended, the degree obtained, the date of graduation, and the major and minors studied. However, this section can be expanded to include awards won and honors achieved. For example:

Harvard University
MBA, International Management, 2007
Dean's List

Iona College
BA, Political Science, 2004

The reverse chronological format is also used in this section. It is appropriate to list any non-matriculated course or additional training taken in a similar format after the traditional education.

Quick Tips
- Unless you are currently pursuing your college degree it is considered amateurish to list high school credits.

- Although it is common to include the date of graduation, this is not a requirement. If you feel the date (recent or not) will leave the reader with an inaccurate perception of you, feel free to leave it off. The important thing is that you earned a specific degree from a specific school.
- Unless you are right out of school (and often even then), few hiring managers care about your GPA.

Other Areas to Include

Of course, you may have other areas of note that are not covered by the main sections described above. The details of these accomplishments can be contained in the following sections:

Skills

If you are seeking a technical job, as in the programmer example above, you should list the equipment, computer languages, and software with which you are familiar. Also be sure to list the languages in which you are fluent.

Publications/Speeches Delivered

Publications convey excellent written communication skills, while speeches provide proof of competence in the verbal component. Including one important example implies that you have done more. Be sure to include your most recent and relevant examples. If you have spoken to the United Nations, there is no need to mention the speech you gave at a neighborhood watch meeting.

Organization Memberships

List organizations related to the work you are seeking and whether you hold an office. Do not list irrelevant ones, as the employer may wonder when you have time to work.

Part 5: Resume Formats

There are three categories of resumes: chronological, functional, and targeted. Each serves a specific purpose and therefore has a different structure. The right format for you depends on your professional background and career objectives. Regardless of the format, your resume has the same purpose: to clearly communicate your professional credentials and exclude any information that is irrelevant or counterproductive.

Chronological

The chronological resume is by far the most common type. It highlights a candidate's employment history sequentially, starting with the most recent experience. When you organize your resume chronologically, the "Career History" section dominates the resume and is placed in the most prominent slot, immediately following your contact information and professional summary. You develop this section by listing your jobs, beginning with the most recent position and working backward toward earlier jobs. Under each listing you describe your responsibilities and accomplishments, giving the most space to the more recent positions.

Many employers prefer the chronological approach. It is especially appropriate if you have a strong employment history with no gaps and are aiming for a position that builds on your current career path.

Functional

A functional resume is organized around a set of skills and accomplishments. It is designed to stress individual areas of competence and is useful for those just entering the job market, those who want to redirect their careers, and those who have little continuous career-related experience.

In this format your employers and academic credentials are listed lower in the document, yielding prime space to projects completed. Often this type of resume cites or is accompanied by sample work product. Examples include links to published clips for writers or completed projects for designers.

Targeted

The targeted resume is a combination of the two previous formats. It is designed to focus attention on what you can do for a specific employer in a specific position. The professional summary still holds the prime spot, but is immediately followed by a list of related capabilities and sample achievements or projects that support your assertion. Employers and schools are listed in subordinate sections.

Targeted resumes are a good choice for people who have a clear idea of what they want to do and can demonstrate their ability in the targeted area. It is a helpful format for those early in a career or those switching professions, as it focuses more on work product than job title and company.

Examples

The following are examples of the resume formats described above.

Chronological

John Doe, Ph.D.
123 Bob Hope Drive
New York, NY 10801

Phone: (555)-555-5555
email: xxxx@aaa.com

PROFESSIONAL SUMMARY

An experienced researcher, analyst, and technical writer with proven abilities to quickly grasp new information and concepts. A seasoned public speaker with the ability to exceed client expectations. Excellent communicator with foreign language abilities in Spanish, Portuguese, and Japanese.

CAREER HISTORY:

University of Wherever, New York, NY, 2011–Present
Instructor

Developed and taught courses in American History that incorporated new insights in the field and included special projects to facilitate learning. Counseled students regarding their educational needs. Key accomplishments include:

- Incorporated Internet technology into course requirements, allowing students to discuss readings and assignments in online discussion forums.
- Created a website for the students to enhance learning. Contains links to course material and related current events.

International Action Network, New York, NY, 2010
Contract Consultant

Researched and wrote briefings on a variety of historical topics. Established and corresponded with contacts in Latin America. Contributed to organization newsletters, grant proposals, and website. Reports demonstrated sensitivity to political and controversial issues. Key accomplishments include:

- Quickly acquired knowledge about comparative global criminal systems and community-based programs. Researched prevention in Central America. Developed a framework for classifying projects in the region.

- Expanded the initial framework to incorporate a more diverse selection of organizations and projects in Latin America and India. Report demonstrated why funding must continue.

University of Wherever, New York, NY, 2003–2009
Ph.D. Student

Researched and wrote papers using a range of writing styles, analytical techniques, and sources in four languages (English, Spanish, Portuguese, and Japanese). Presented scholarly work at various regional and international conferences. Passed Ph.D. examinations with distinction.

- Conceptualized, researched, and wrote a 300-page analysis of the political impact of the initial highway network, demonstrated how the Institutional Revolutionary Party used road construction to entrench itself in Mexican politics and society.

Bob's Data, New York, NY, 2002
Administrative Assistant

Provided administrative support to three departments and several programming teams. Key accomplishments include:

- Identified needs and developed an internal cost-tracking system. Programmed Excel to extract data from employees' electronic timesheets and then create graphs to illustrate cost overruns on programmer time. Helped company to improve accuracy on internal costs when negotiating with clients.

Accident Research Team, New York, NY, 2000–2002
Research Assistant

- Completed defect and collision investigations, located damaged vehicles and documented damage, assessed accident scenes, acquired medical reports and coded the injuries listed, reported to transport officials, liaised with police officers and auto wreckers, interviewed accident casualties, and wrote summary reports.
- Initiated and wrote a pamphlet on automotive consumer rights and issues; coordinated a special study on the effects of photo radar on traffic patterns.

EDUCATION
University of Wherever
Ph.D., History, 2009 (Modern Latin American and World History)

University of Wherever
M.A. (Honors), History, 2004

University of Wherever
B.A. (Honors), History, 2000

SELECTED PUBLICATIONS
- "Solving Occupant Safety." (Technical Conference on Vehicle Safety, New York, NY, January 2014).
- "Revolutionizing Roads." *Journal of Safety History* 35, no. 3 (2013): 245–264

COMPUTER SKILLS
Microsoft Word, Excel, Project, Adobe Photoshop, and HTML

MEMBERSHIPS
Canadian Council for the Americas, British Columbia Chapter
Vancouver Institute for the Americas

Functional

Gail X
123 Lois Lane
Smallville, Kansas 66684

Phone: 555-221-1234
Email: xxx@aaa.com

Objective: To obtain a position as a Microsoft Office Specialist trainer

Skills Summary

- Presentation Skills
- Certified Project Manager
- Certified MS Professional
- Course Design and Development
- Graphic Artist
- Published Writer

Presentation Experience

- Created and delivered real estate not-for-profit tax seminars throughout Kansas, which saved a collection of local groups in excess of $30 million.
- Served as president of Toastmasters, earned the level of Competent Communicator.
- Delivered over 200 speeches in a 10-year period. Earned numerous best-speaker awards. Competed in area speech contests.

Computer Skills

- MS Word
- PowerPoint
- Excel
- Access

Course Design

Developed a seminar, "Speeding Bullet Change," designed to help average citizens navigate city bureaucracy. Information included how to obtain a building permit and other various licenses, and how to proceed in small claims court.

Management

Managed special events and public speaking appearances for three Kansas mayors, including broadcast appearances, public ceremonies, receptions, parades, and community appearances.

Education

- NY College Certificate Program in Microsoft Office
- NY University Certificate Courses in Special Events and Meeting Planning

Work Experience

Office of the Mayor, Smallville, Kansas, 2010–2014
Community Liaison and Coordinator

Targeted

Peter Parker
123 Spider Drive
Scarsdale, New York 10583
Phone (555) 287-8512

PROFESSIONAL SUMMARY

Professional project manager with over 15 years' experience in successfully managing large-volume projects. Solid experience in setting and maintaining schedules, prioritizing workloads, and maximizing performance of project teams to complete projects cost-effectively and on time. Strong persuasive and motivational skills.

Key Skills:

- Presentation Skills
- Certified Project Manager
- Experienced Manager

- Program Design and Development
- International Experience
- Published Writer

CAREER HISTORY

1991–2012   **MOVIE CORP—New York, NY**
2007–2012   *Production Manager, Print Services*

- Managed subscriber-acquisition marketing strategies and plans, including a $30 million annual advertising and promotions budget.
- Directed several advertising agencies on network's direct response creative and media tactics, including mail, print, outdoor, and point-of-sale materials.
- Led a 10-person team responsible for developing and executing subscriber acquisition.
- Developed operating-systems procedures for all outside and in-house efforts, resulting in 15% reduction in printing costs.
- Selected and negotiated with outside suppliers for creative/production services and shipping of over $10 million in marketing materials.

2002–2007	*Senior Manager, Print Production*

- Managed outside creative services in addition to six print production department staff.
- Planned and reviewed with each employee company guidelines for preparation of pre-press and manufacturing of all creatives.
- Coordinated deadlines with in-house staff and external sources, resulting in producing and delivering materials in one-third less time than the scheduled negotiation.

1997–2001	*Manager, Print Department*

- Produced collateral material.
- Attended press runs, evaluated progress and manufacturing bids, and selected vendors based on company guidelines and criteria.
- Managed a staff of three.

1193–1997	*Assistant Production Manager*

- Prepared artwork, corrected color, and formatted for size efficiencies to ensure successful design results.
- Managed a staff of two.

1991–1992	*Production Assistant*

- Purchased two- and four-color promotional material.
- Attended press runs and organized completion of programs.

AWARDS

Received 15 awards from the American Graphics Association for specialty printing.

PROFESSIONAL AFFILIATIONS

- Cable Television Association of Marketers
- American Graphics Association
- National Association of Minorities in Communication

EDUCATION
University of Wherever
B.A. History, 1992

Part 6: Resume Review

Test Yourself

We are almost through with Phase 2 – Building a Rock Star Resume. Before you set out to craft the final version of your resume, take a few moments to analyze the sample below. If you were the recruiter or hiring manager, how would you react to this document? How can it be improved?

Brian

2518 New Road

Highlands, NY 99000

(999) 555-8456

Objective: My intent is to find a position with a progressive, energetic organization that will utilize my Human Resource skills and joy of Management.

Experience: Big Corp., West Point, NY - Government Contract #347- BCD-82.36

SSI Services Inc., West Point, NY- Government Contract #ABC - 968

1997-Present

Operations Manager: Direct a 24hr/365day motor-pool dispatch office and all related activities needed to support the United Stats Military Academy's personnel such as; community transit system, fuel and water delivery, overseeing and training a Union staff of 5.

- Actively involved in negotiations with the Collective Bargaining Agreement of 1999.
- Revised payment system for Holiday pay in alignment with the GSA at a 20% cost loss
- Devised and implemented New Employee Orientation Program.

1994-1997

Fleet Supervisor: Scheduled a 600 large tactical/commercial fleet and 75 Drivers to satisfy the customers needs in the most economical manner.

- Developed the transportation and lodging for personnel to support the Official/Athletic needs of the United Military Academy. And I Planned travel.

1993-1994

Assistant Fleet Supervisor: Provided support to Operations, to include payroll and billing.

- Revamped format of company documents to enhance compilation of data.

Office Machine Repair Coordinator and Production Control Specialist: Facilitated repairs of computer hardware and tactical/commercial vehicles for the customer.

Education	Please Have Mercy College, Dobbs Ferry, NY
	Masters of Science in
	BS is Basket Weaving
Computer Skills	MS Office, Windows, and Internet
Affiliations	Society for Human Resource Management - National

Mid-Hudson Valley

Coach Exercise 7: Reviewing the Sample

Okay, so maybe that was a bit much, but submitting a poorly designed resume is like sending a "don't hire me" telegram to a prospective employer. Take a few moments to discuss your findings with your career coach. Did you find all the mistakes? Hopefully you don't have any of these errors in your document.

"Resume Rights" – A Quick Guide

The following is a quick summary that will help you keep all these lessons in mind as you draft your resume.

PROFESSIONAL SUMMARY:

Three or four sentences that describe what you do and, in turn, what you can offer the hiring organization. No, not "I'm a Taurus and enjoy long walks on the beach ..." Something more like "A certified facilitator with advanced computer skills. An experienced course designer with ..." You get the idea.

CAREER HISTORY:

Company: City, State – 2013–Present
Optional: Description of company, e.g., A global manufacturing company with 25,000 employees
Your Title

This is where you include a general job description listing your major responsibilities and accountabilities. At the end of this description, which should use action verbs, you will note your **key accomplishments** (CAR statements).

- Now tell me about a specific time you rose above your basic job description, stepped in for your manager, **raised production**, lowered costs, etc.
- If you have another one, list it as well.
- Be sure to **bold** what you want to stand out. These should be items of particular interest to the employer – the key words that match their needs. If you're computer savvy, take time to consider which descriptors search engines would most likely flag, and incorporate those as well.

2010–2014   **Company**, City, State
                   Your title
                   Here is another format for the experience section—one that offers more white space. Regardless of which you select, include the same type of information for this job. Make sure that everything is spelled correctly. How will you feel if you are the last one to notice that a word is spelled wrong?

- Remember that brevity is key. This bullet must describe the **challenging** situation, the **action** you took to resolve it, and the **result** you achieved. Use data when possible.

EDUCATION:

2005–2009   **School**, City, State

Degree:

If you are early in your career, you may also want to note your major and any applicable awards or distinctions, e.g., dean's list, honors, GPA.

COMPUTER SKILLS:

Now you can list all those nifty programs: Word, Excel, Access, PowerPoint, Etch A Sketch (just kidding!), PageMaker, etc.

PUBLICATIONS:

"My Career Coach Is a Genius." Article published in the *Plotline Leadership Journal of Awesome*, 2014.

AWARDS:

"Whatever Award." Presented by Plotline Leadership, 2013.

Resume Quick Check

The days of employees spending their entire careers at one company are long gone. Today's workers will likely changes jobs more than five times and change careers two or more times. Therefore, it is a good idea to continuously update your resume.

Coach Exercise 8: The Final Check

To ensure your resume is producing the desired result, ask your career coach to review the revised document with the following points in mind:

Positioning

- If I spend just thirty seconds looking at the resume, what concepts and ideas jump out?
- Which job titles, degrees, and company names come through?
- How is the candidate positioned by the resume? What message do I take away?
- Are there any red flags, such as employment gaps, that will need to be addressed?
- Does the resume clearly indicate what the person does and how that will benefit your company?

Objective/Professional Summary

- Does it provide a comprehensive description of the candidate's experiences and qualifications without being wordy?
- Do statements that differentiate the person from other candidates follow the section?
- Does it include a statement or two that gives the reader an indication of the candidate's personality or his/her approach to the work?

Experience/Accomplishments

- Did the candidate simply provide a historical list of responsibilities and achievements or did he/she call out specific CAR-based accomplishments that align to the job description/employer needs?
- Did the candidate include relevant accomplishments such as volunteer activities, performance awards, and applicable speaking and writing activities?
- Did the highlighted CAR statement showcase an appropriate balance between team-based and individual projects? Is the candidate's role clear in all cases?
- Are the accomplishments easy to read?
  - Bulleted rather than long paragraphs
  - Short phrases and action words
  - Measurable and specific
  - Relevant to the job sought

Professional Appearance

- **White space:** Is there enough?
- **Length:** Is the resume as short as possible while still telling his/her story?
- **Writing Style:** Can the reader understand the point he/she is trying to make in each statement?
- **Clarity:** Did he/she state things clearly, so the reader will come away with the right message?
- **Completeness:** Is all the important information included? Have all dates been accounted for?
- **Typos:** Is the resume error-free?

Final Draft

Now that you have the tools, put them to use by completing the final draft of your resume. If you haven't already secured a career coach, log on to www.plotlineleadership.com to learn more about how we can help you directly or facilitate a productive connection.

If your resume is in great shape, it's time to focus on the interview process. In the next phase, "Becoming a Master Interviewee," we will help you polish your skills and secure the job of your dreams.

Resume Submission – A Word on LinkedIn

Before moving to the final section, I need to briefly touch on the use of LinkedIn. Since its initial release, the site has grown considerably in both use and influence. These days professionals at all levels – regardless of their job-hunting status – are expected to have an online presence. In many ways the LinkedIn profile has replaced the business card and contact database as a way to stay connected with other professionals.

This is most evident at conferences, where people exchange LinkedIn connection requests as often, or more frequently, than they do business cards. The tool can be extremely helpful in building and maintaining a network, attracting the attention of recruiters, and providing a forum to share one's expertise and business wins. But like any tool, it's only effective when you use it correctly. There are books and white papers devoted to the subject, but you should at least keep these three points in mind.

1. **Be Consistent** – The LinkedIn profile is in many ways a mini resume, so ensure there is consistency between what you say on your profile and what you have on your document. A few years ago a staffing colleague of mine caught a senior-level candidate fudging her online presence. The incongruent statements were vetted in the interview process and the person, an otherwise capable professional, was passed over from the role. Integrity matters!

2. **Be Respectful** – No one likes junk mail. When you mindlessly click the *connect* button, you instantly lose credibility. Have a reason for requesting the connection and express that via a personalized note to the recipient. I'm more apt to accept a request from someone I haven't actually met if they offer a valid reason for the connection. Examples include the student looking for an internship, the new coach looking for tips on the business, or a struggling writer seeking advice. Sure, I'd be *even more* likely to respond if you have something to offer – e.g., a consulting, coaching, or speaking request. The world is small and karma works, so it's a smart policy to help those who reach out for assistance. Remember, the more you give, the more you get.

3. **Be Professional** – LinkedIn isn't Facebook, and it's certainly not Match.com. Keep your posts business-oriented, avoid rants and inflammatory language, and avoid being the "creepy guy/girl" by resisting the temptation to cyber-stalk that cute colleague. (This actually happens!) Also, whether you agree with the view, in many ways your online actions reflect on your current employer. Be mindful of the connection and act accordingly.

Phase 3 – Becoming A Master Interviewee

Purpose

In today's job market it takes more than a smile and stock answers to land the perfect position. Furthermore, while having a well-crafted resume may open opportunity's door, being properly prepared for the interviewing process can ensure that it's not slammed in your face.

Description

This phase is designed to help the career-minded navigate any interview. Whether you're looking to change jobs, switch careers, or simply gauge your current value through informational interviews, these techniques will help you succeed. Specifically, this phase will help you:

- Understand the importance of the pre-interview process
- Adapt and respond to any interview format or structure
- Gain awareness of possible pre-employment tests or assessments
- Open the interview effectively by gaining and maintaining rapport with the interviewer
- Obtain the objectives of the interview and hiring process
- Control the pace and tone of the interview
- Read, analyze, and evaluate an interviewer's body language
- Read, analyze, and evaluate an interviewer's verbal cues
- Answer various question types, including those on stress, behavior, and situation
- Ask effective questions of the interviewer
- Obtain feedback from the interviewer
- Understand the importance of the post-interview process

Introduction

These days there is no nine-to-five job. Thanks to advances in technology, employees have the *opportunity* to work around the clock – an expectation that only increases for those who are employed by global organizations. People work during traditional office hours, while in transit, and – more frequently than ever – bookend their days with even more company time, thanks to the proliferation of home offices. More than ever, people are identifying with their positions and, in turn, those positions are having a profound effect on their personal lives.

Securing the right job is the easiest way to ensure a productive, healthy coexistence between work and personal life. Conversely, obtaining the wrong position can produce a host of costly consequences, including depression, stress, and a variety of physical ailments, not to mention the costs associated with searching for a new job.

So what separates success and failure in this endeavor?
What makes an interview productive or disastrous?

Simply put, most job applicants underestimate the breadth of skills required to navigate the interview process.

Many people tend to overestimate their interviewing skill. Do you? Before answering, consider a related observation, which notes that over 85 percent of people consider themselves above-average drivers. That's mathematically impossible! And it's just as unlikely that you will do well on an interview without proper preparation and ample practice.

This final phase explores the art and science of interviewing and will help you recognize and master its intricacies. The combination of discussion, role-play, and interactive exercises will help you perform well throughout an interview. It examines your experiences, analyzes your verbal and nonverbal communication skills, and demonstrates how to gain and maintain rapport with the interviewer. At the conclusion of this phase, you should feel confident enough to perform effectively in any setting.

Introverts, this is where we're going to get serious, so grab a helmet. If you've done your prep work, the prospect of dealing with interview, especially the dreaded panel interview, should be easier to take. That said, it's always nerve-racking.

Part 1: Ice Breaker

Interview Readiness Assessment

Any seasoned trainer or career coach will tell you that skill assessment is critical to the learning process. Knowing your current level of competency in a given subject will help you focus on specific learning outcomes, allowing you to both leverage your strengths and minimize your weaknesses.

This learning strategy, which is known as **deliberate practice**, can help you get better at specific interviewing skills without wasting time belaboring what you already understand and can effectively demonstrate. An objective, experienced third party such as an executive career coach or mentor can also help you notice bad habits or "blind spots" (e.g., the classic spinach in the teeth) that can stand in the way of your success.

Although this phase is written for individual participants, you will get even more out of the work by reviewing the exercises with your career coach. If you'd like more information on career coaching, visit www.plotlineleadership.com. For now, let's begin with a trial interview.

Coach Exercise 9: Mock Interview

Instructions

1. Ask your career coach to engage in a mock interview.
2. Briefly describe your career background. Sample backstories include:
    - You are seeking a position as a customer service representative. You are without a college education, but have two years of relevant experience. You are reliable and friendly, and can complete work in a quick, organized fashion.
    - You are an MBA with fifteen years of experience in corporate business-to-business sales who would like to transition into sales management. You've managed small teams earlier in your career in a marketing role, but haven't done so in over a decade.
    - Insert your story here:

Your Story

_____

_____

_____

_____

_____

_____

3. For the purpose of this exercise, your coach will play the role of the interviewer. Spend ten minutes answering his or her interview questions.

4. **Debrief**: Discuss the "cold interview." Ask your coach to provide feedback on the way you answered the questions. Input can include such topics as verbal and nonverbal communication, professionalism, and ability to keep focused on skills.

An Interview's Purpose

Professional resume writers, online research, and computer-driven templates make it easy for candidates to shine on paper. A good interviewer knows this and will be looking for those who can effectively rise above the "cookie-cutter" candidates.

An interview helps the hiring manager confirm that the skills promised on the resume will be fulfilled if you are selected for a role. It also gives you an opportunity to display your personality and helps shape the interviewer's opinions as to whether you fit with the organization's culture.

Part 2: Preparing the Process

Preparing for Various Interview Formats

An interviewer has a number of formats from which to select. The decision will largely depend on the type of position, the corporate culture, and the objectives of the hiring manager. Therefore, you should be comfortable with each one. While there are many types of interviews, most are structured and feature planned questions and a set style. The most common include:

The Screening Interview

The screen is a fundamental part of the interview process. It is designed to weed out those who appear qualified on paper, but ultimately may not be. Because there are usually many candidates at this stage, it is important to differentiate yourself. To ensure effectiveness:

- Quickly ascertain the purpose of the interview.
- Briefly answer all direct close-ended questions that are meant to confirm, or call into question, assertions made on your resume.
- Be ready for well-formed open-ended questions designed to test technical knowledge, industry awareness, or general communication skills.
- Inquire about the company's hiring process, the timeframe, and who is responsible for the hiring decision.
- Ask about their preferred method of follow-up and be sure to do so.
- Ask for feedback if rejected. Note: Most organizations, given the risk of potential discrimination-oriented legal claims, will not provide debriefing sessions. However, it doesn't hurt to ask.

The Telephone Interview

This is a cost-effective, time-saving format that also helps reduce the risk of personal bias. It can replace the traditional screening interview as the first step in the hiring process. To perform well on a telephone interview:

- Answer the call from a quiet setting.
- While this rarely happens, if you are asked to call the interviewer, be on time!

- Keep your resume and CAR statements handy.
- Be friendly – smiles come through on the phone.
- Get settled beforehand, so you can avoid sounding preoccupied or, worse, unintelligent. Sit quietly and wait for the call. Do not get caught up in another activity.
- Practice active listening.
- Stand up if you feel yourself drifting.
- Ask at least one or two well-formed questions.
- Ask about the follow-up procedures.

The Task-Oriented Interview

This format requires you to perform some small project or submit sample work in order to qualify for the main interview. Tasks can range from writing samples to projects done on spec. This may be incorporated into the larger interview process. For example, when applying for a position as a trainer, you may be asked in a later interview to perform a "teach back," a short lesson that demonstrates your skills in front of a classroom.

The Video Interview

Advances in technology have helped HR departments and recruiting companies meet the budget-tightening demands of their leadership. Thanks to some savvy software, hiring managers can record key questions in a single sitting and then review the answers of select candidates at their leisure. The new systems not only save travel expenses and reduce administrative burden, they also decrease the time managers need to spend on the process.

Video interviews can't replace actual interaction, but many larger companies are using these tools for high-volume roles at the earlier stages of the screening process. These interviews, while skewing to more basic inquiries, can include a variety of question formats. Therefore, it pays to get familiar with both the technology and your ability to effectively express yourself via the medium.

The Behavioral Interview

One of the more popular formats, the behavioral-based interview, allows the interviewer to isolate and examine your experiences in specific areas by requiring you to provide specific examples of how you have handled various situations and demonstrated relevant skills. *Please note: Interviewers will usually not tell you what competencies they are looking for.*

This is an area that introverts typically dread, but if you have completed the exercises in the prior phase, you should be well prepared. It's a good idea to review your relevant CAR statements before the interview so you have powerful "war stories" on tap to align with potential questions.

Coach Exercise 10: Behavioral Interview Questions

The following table lists a number of topics/competencies that are commonly discussed using the behavioral interview format. For each topic, your coach can ask you a behavior-based question. Try your hand at giving answers. **Note:** *Common follow-up questions are listed after the main question in each category. This is key, as many interviewers will pepper candidates with several questions (or ask related ones in quick succession) to ensure a topic is fully explored.*

Ask your coach to provide brief constructive feedback regarding your responses. If you don't have a coach, simply record your answers and discuss with a mentor or trusted colleague. Make sure you were able to answer the initial question and any related follow-ups.

Topic/ Competency	Fill In Your Answers Below
Conflict Resolution	Q: Have you ever effectively resolved a conflict between yourself and a colleague or manager? If so, what process/techniques did you use? How did you arrive at a compromise? A:
Organization and Planning	Q: Have you ever been charged with organizing an event or project? If so, how did you develop and implement your plan? A:

Topic/ Competency	Fill In Your Answers Below
Communication and Presentation	Q: When in your career were you responsible for communicating to a large group? How did you prepare for and deliver the presentation? Do you change your style to accommodate the specific audience? How? A:
Problem-Solving	Q: Provide an example of a time when you provided an innovative solution to a pressing problem. How did you arrive at the answer? How did you get support for and implement the solutions? A:
Decision-Making	Q: Were you ever responsible for making a key decision in your department? If so, how did you go about identifying alternatives and making your final selection? A:
Team-Building	Q: Have you ever acted as a leader in your department? How have you gone about producing a team-based effort in a new project? A:
Creativity	Q: Describe a time when you took an innovative/creative approach to a challenging problem. What process did you use to "think outside the box"? A:
Motivating Others	Q: When have you had to motivate a group of stakeholders? How did you motivate people of different personality types? Follow-up: What motivates you? A:
Stress/Deadline Management	Q: Give an example of a time you worked under a tight deadline and did not meet the mark. What prevented you from meeting your obligation? What did you learn? A:

Remember, it's always best to use examples from actual work to showcase how you leveraged the competency in question. Also, be clear as to what your role was on the project. Mentioning the team highlights your ability to collaborate, but make sure your voice is heard and your contributions are noted.

Bonus Points: The examples in Coach Exercise 10 above reference behavioral competencies. Similar examples can be used for industry-specific skills and projects. If you are seeking a job that requires such skills ask your coach to help you explore these areas to ensure you are prepared to provide compelling, specific, complete answers. A sample framework is noted below.

Topic/Skill	Fill In Your Answers Below
Technical Skills	Q: How would you incorporate your knowledge of XXX into this position if you were hired? Tell me about a time when you made a similar transition. A:
Software Skills	Q: Your resume indicates you have experience in XXX software program. How would you use this on a daily basis to achieve better business results? A:

Double Bonus Points: The examples can be personalized even further to explore the requirements and needs of the specific position sought. Consider the sample below, which describes a generic competency, but in terms of how it is applied within a specific role – in this case, a proposal developer. If you really want to prepare for a behavioral-based interview, consider what is key to the role, confirm the competency definitions, and then work with your career coach to frame questions like the ones below.

Topic/Competency	Key Questions
Planning • Accurately scopes length and difficulty of tasks and projects • Sets objectives and goals, breaks down work into process steps • Develops schedules and assignments • Anticipates and adjusts for problems and	1. Proposal developers work under tight deadlines. Give an example of how your planning/project-management process helped ensure multiple deliverables were completed on time. 2. Can you provide an example of having to juggle multiple customer requests? How did you handle the competing priorities to ensure all needs were met? 3. Proposal developers are often reliant on the input of others. Can you provide an example of time when you had to plan for securing input from several parties? How did you ensure all input arrived on time?

roadblocks, measures performance against goals, evaluates results	4. Describe a situation in which your planning process broke down. What did you learn? What changes have you made to your process to ensure you don't fall into similar situations in the future?

Insight: As a career coach and corporate executive I'm constantly helping people find balance. In some cases, this involves ensuring their humble nature doesn't overshadow the impact they've had. In other cases, it involves helping ambitious people avoid the tendency to overplay their hand. Sharing credit and/or highlighting others will balance your drive with much-needed corporate collaboration.

Sidebar for HR Pros and Hiring Managers

- As an Organization Development consultant, I've worked with many leaders to frame both role profiles that describe excellence in a position and tools to ensure the best possible people are hired or promoted. Many companies use these tools to reduce the costs and complications that come from a bad hire.
- If your organization would like more information on how to design an effective role profile for a given position or insights on the buy vs. build decision for related assessments, contact us via www.plotlineleadership.com.

The Panel Interview

The panel interview allows the interviewer to introduce you to a segment of your prospective work group. It also lets them test your skill in small group communication. This timesaving format allows potential colleagues and the HR representative to ask a variety of general questions in a single session. To be successful:

- Quickly identify the lead interviewer.
- Collect business cards from all panelists. Lay them on the table to help you remember names.
- Use their names.
- Try to get a sense of who does what (regardless of title) and who will make the ultimate hiring decision.
- Be prepared for, and answer, all follow-up questions.

- Don't interrupt an interviewer.
- Answer all relevant questions.
- Ask clarifying questions, if necessary.
- Do not be afraid to redirect the conversation if the panelists get off track.
- Look directly at the person asking the question while he or she is doing so, but focus on the entire group when answering questions.
- Control the pace of the dialogue.
- Thank them for their time.

The Team Interview

This format also allows several staff members to question you, but in this case they do so individually, in consecutive one-on-one sessions. This allows each person to form a separate opinion of you while asking questions relevant to their area of expertise. Keep in mind that there is likely to be overlap between the sections, so be sure to remain consistent. Honesty and character are key. To be successful:

- Inquire about the process, i.e., identify who you will be talking to, how long each segment will last, and whether you will need multiple interview sessions.
- Determine or confirm the specific coverage areas for each interviewer – what's important to him or her?
- Gain rapport with each person by noting his or her communication style and body language. Use the **mirror, match, and lead** technique (explained below) to set the pace.
- Be aware that you will likely be judged by both subjective opinions and an objective, position-based criteria system.
- Focus on the needs of each member without making assumptions. You might be tempted to talk technology with IT and people skills with the HR person, but this could backfire. Treat people as individuals, not titles.
  - **Insight**: The mirror, match, and lead technique noted above is a way to gain rapport with a person on a subconscious level. It involves aligning your nonverbal and verbal cues to those of your counterpart. When done well, it gives the other person the impression that you are "in sync." This technique has three basic elements:

- o **Mirror** – Align your presence to that of your interviewer. For example, if they sit straight and take notes, don't slouch and stair idly at your empty hands.
- o **Match** – Subtly assume their pace, tone, and movement signature. For example, if they are animated, talk quickly, and speak with enthusiasm, don't put them to sleep with a demeanor that is too reserved.
- o **Lead** – Once you are deep in the conversation, test your level of rapport by shifting something small, e.g., your tone or posture, and see if they follow. For example, lowering your voice and leaning in is an excellent way to test the level of interest during the close.
    - Just picture, at the conclusion of a successful interview, leaning in and asking the interviewer, "Do you know what?" and having him or her, lean in, voice mirroring yours, and asking, "What?"
    - If you said, at that moment, "I think I'd do some great work in this role" (or another comment that expresses sincere interest in the position), you'd create a memorable X factor moment that could distinguish you from other candidates.
    - Will this technique get you the job on its own? Probably not. But relationship (fit factor) is an important decision criterion so, all things being equal, having this level of mastery over communication could help swing things in your favor.
- Keep in mind that this is an advanced negotiation technique. There are a number of excellent books on neuro-linguistic programming (NLP) – the science behind the strategy. Ask your coach about its usefulness in the interview close and salary negotiation process.

The Stress Interview

This interview type is traditionally used for various government and law-enforcement positions. Though rare in the corporate setting, depending on the position and company culture, elements of the technique can worm their way into your next interview.

Designed to test your behavior, logic, and control under pressure, this format is most useful for selecting employees for high-pressure positions, from customer service representative to air traffic controller. To perform well on a stress interview:

- Realize that they will never tell you that you are undergoing a stress interview. However, it will become clear within a few minutes.
- Don't be afraid of silence. They will try to use the power of silence by remaining quiet after you answer a question. Don't cave in and feel compelled to give additional information. Remain quiet until they ask another question or move to the next topic.
- Be patient and professional.
- Stick to the purpose of the interview.
- Be prepared for:
  - Rapid questions
  - Irrelevant questions
  - The same question asked in different ways
  - Distractions, including phone, email alerts, and administrative interruptions
  - Irritating or irrational remarks
  - Criticism of your answers and/or resume format

Your goal in this setting is to stay cool and professional, providing competent, thoughtful answers while attempting to build rapport. It's challenging, to be sure, but it provides the interviewer with an indication of how you conduct yourself under pressure. As noted above, this is critical in roles as diverse as customer service representative and air traffic controller.

The "Tell Me About Yourself" Interview

While this format can appear largely unstructured, the open-ended question style is used to see if you can focus on the task at hand. It also tests your organization and communication skills. To be effective:

- Avoid telling your life story.
- Stick to qualifications and what you can do for their organization.
- Effectively narrow a hiring manager's focus with clarifying questions.

- Take control of the interview process by asking if they need additional information on a particular subject.
- Don't be afraid to redirect a line of questioning.

Remember, not every interviewer knows what he or she is doing. While some (typically from HR) will be experienced interviewers who perform the task as a regular part of their jobs, many hiring managers interview only sporadically and may not be as well versed in the various question types unless recently trained or prepped by their HR business partner.

Often, this "Tell me about yourself" technique is used by inexperienced managers or those who are out of practice. Remember that they might be nervous as well. If you think about it, given the cost of a fully loaded employee (salary, benefits, etc.), hiring someone is a major financial decision. And making bad hire can be a significant blotch on one's career. Anything you can do to put the interviewer at ease and help them see that hiring you would be a smart choice will increase your chances of making a connection.

Understanding Preemployment Tests

Even the most highly trained interviewers are still human. To guard against making a poor hiring decision, they often complement their subjective analysis with a preemployment test and/or other assessments. You must be prepared to deal with each type. Options include:

Personality Tests

Popular tools such as the Myers-Briggs Type Indicator (MBTI), DiSC, and Personal Styles Inventory help determine your general personality (usually in terms of defined character types, e.g., Introverted vs. Extroverted), and thus whether you would be a good fit for their organization or department. Employers understand, however, that such tests are only useful in determining a general trend or set of characteristics.

Aptitude Tests

These tools are traditionally used to help employers identify basic deficiencies (or abilities) in a candidate's reading comprehension, mathematics, or writing skills. However, higher-level tests, measuring cognitive reasoning, problem solving, critical thinking, and overall intelligence are also used. The Wonderlic Cognitive Ability Test is a popular example. Try to find out ahead of time whether you will be subjected to such tests. Usually there is not much you can do to prepare for them, but it's good to avoid surprises where possible.

Functional Skills Tests

Functional tests measure your ability in various programs and procedures directly related to a particular position. They are especially useful in determining the accuracy of information alleged on your resume. A basic example is typing speed or proficiency in a particular computer program. At higher levels it could be programming language or a "teach back" to demonstrate presentation skills.

Behavior-Based Tests

Built on the theory that human behavior is repetitive and constant, these tools help predict the likelihood of your success in a particular role. Given their predictive nature, these tests are typically validated and used to simply *inform* the hiring decisions rather than offer a gating point or "go/no-go" decision.

Many assessment companies build role profiles for specific job classifications such as sales, and then design or select vendor-developed tests to predict whether applicants will meet the required level of success for each competency associated with the profile. While there are many stock tests on the market, savvy HR professionals will ensure the tests align to their specific needs.

Situational Tests

This is a hands-on test that temporarily places you in the working environment to gauge reaction, adaptation, performance, and ability. Due to the expense and time requirement, these are rarely used for external hires. More often these form part of a larger assessment program and are used to evaluate a cadre of high-potential employees. That said, due to their effectiveness, many consulting organizations are developing shorter versions of these assessment centers – some of which can be conducted online, over the phone, or via virtual asynchronous portals to test the skills of a prospective employee.

Testing Guidelines

You will typically be forewarned about the time and nature of the test. In addition, to ensure the accuracy, validity, and usefulness of these measures, test facilitators observe a set of testing guidelines. Thus, tests must be:

- Administered by a trained professional
- Kept confidential – clear data-sharing rules must be communicated in advance
- Properly explained and held in a consistent, and preferably comfortable, setting
- Designed by a reputable source and meet specific validity criteria
- Updated and reviewed regularly

- Considered a complement to the interview – they should make up only a portion of the evaluation
- Aligned to local data-protection rules (within Europe)

As a candidate, it is important to understand that you have the right to know:

- Why the organization is using the test
- What it is designed to measure
- What impact or weighting it will have on the hiring decision
- Who will see the results
- If the results will be retained and, if so, for how long

Part 3: Opening the Interview

Prepare Yourself

The following suggestions may appear basic to the experienced professional. However, it's important to remember that most workers, especially successful corporate employees, don't often find themselves in a position to have to formally interview for a job.

Leveraging your network to score a promotion while gainfully employed is different from hitting the bricks as an outsider when there's no paycheck coming in. When you're stressed it's easy to overlook the little things like that loose change jangling in your pocket and your vibrating mobile phone. Deal breakers? Probably not, but why have the distraction during a conversation?

Note for Introverts: If you are like me (and many other introverts), you have a tendency to get "stuck in your head." Because we often have a strong internal frame of reference and focus more on content than context, we can sometimes overlook the outward-facing, and perhaps superficial, elements of our presence. Make sure you take time to consider how you come across (look and sound) to people who don't know you.

Regardless of your introvert/extrovert profile, initial meetings can be disconcerting when a job is on the line. Your comfort and confidence are critical to your success. To ensure you look, act, and feel like a professional, observe the following:

- Turn off your mobile phone before entering the building.
- Gather needed material and briefly review your resume and CAR statements.
- Adjust your clothing and neaten your hair … breath mint, anyone?
- Enjoy a moment of silence to focus on the task at hand.
- Mind your shoes. As superficial as it sounds, if you want an interviewer to "take a shine to you," start with your footwear. As you will see in the final phase, "Tips from the Trenches," several of the staffing professional interviewed for this book thought enough about the topic to afford it a mention, and these folks are rock stars in the field.

Gaining Rapport with the Interviewer

Applicants are expected to be nervous before an interview. But believe it or not, many interviewers – even seasoned professionals – also get the jitters beforehand, and it is to your advantage to put them at ease. A relaxed interviewer will better represent their organization and be able to focus clearly on your skills and experiences. You can make a strong impression by doing the following:

- Demonstrate respect by standing to greet the interviewer.
- Offer a firm handshake and smile.
- Greet him or her by name and maintain eye contact.
- And as challenging as this may be for my fellow introverts, begin with small talk to set a relaxed tone. The little things matter, so scan their office for cues or subtle ways to navigate the chitchat phase. These often include sports memorabilia, hobby-related knickknacks, or more formal role-related awards and degrees.
  - o **Note**: Be sure to adjust this approach to align with expected cultural norms if searching for a position outside your home country or geography.

Understanding Hiring Process Objectives

If you are currently employed and in the process of interviewing with several organizations, time constraints will be of major importance. To keep on pace while maintaining a positive flow, do the following:

- Before you go, ask for an estimated interview length and/or note any time restrictions.
- If unclear, ask for the purpose of the interview and/or stage of the search (are you the first person in, the last person to be interviewed, the start of a rebooted process, or somewhere in between?). The added detail can help you ask intelligent follow-up questions.
- If you are to meet with more than one person, obtain their name, title, and affiliation with the open position.
- Ask if this is to be the first of several interviews.
- Ask for an estimation of when they will make a hiring decision.

Coach Exercise 11: Interview Introduction

Now that you know the secrets of setting the tone and establishing rapport, try it yourself. Ask your coach to walk though an interview introduction. Try to gain rapport while uncovering all needed information.

Part 4: Communicating Throughout the Interview

Controlling the Pace and Tone of the Interview

It is not enough to simply establish rapport with the interviewer. To be effective, you must maintain that rapport and exude the right blend of personality and professionalism throughout the meeting. To do this, try the following:

- Have a clear knowledge of your career highlights and be able to back them up with well-prepared CAR statements.
- Adjust the pace, pitch, and tone of your voice to indicate interest and friendliness.
- Ask clarifying questions if the initial question was vague.
- Offer examples and stories of job-related triumphs to ensure your point is made.
- Display a sense of humor where appropriate.
- Avoid monotone voice patterns and discouraging nonverbal communication like yawning, foot tapping, and rolling of the eyes. (Believe me, this happens even at senior levels!)
- Avoid looking at your watch and mobile phone.

Learning to Listen

It's natural in an interview setting to hyper-focus on what you want to say. Even naturally reserved people can turn chatty out of a desire to convey their qualifications to the hiring manager. But don't underestimate the power of listening. Listening demonstrates your willingness to understand and appreciate the interviewer's needs. It also creates trust in relationships. This is an area where introverts can excel, so be sure to take full advantage of your ability to actively listen to others.

Traditionally, there are five Levels of Listening, ranked below from most to least effective:

- Level 5 – Listening for Complete Understanding: for subtlety; reading between the lines
- Level 4 – Listening for Application: how you can use/build on what was said
- Level 3 – Judgmental Listening: listening for evaluation/a chance to agree or disagree

- Level 2 – Opportunistic Listening: listening simply for a chance to tell your story
- Level 1 – Non-listening: "What was that again?" "Can you repeat that?"

Even under normal circumstances many people have difficulty moving past Level 3. During an interview the compulsion to stay at Level 2 can be very strong. Savvy interviewees, however, realize that often the best way to maintain rapport with and convey your intelligence to an interviewer is to move to Level 4 or 5 during the course of the conversation.

Self-Guided Exercise 24: Gauge Your Current Level of Listening

The following evaluation will give you an indication of your current ability to listen.

	Listening Skills Assign each question a number **4 = Almost Always 3 = Usually 2 = Sometimes 1 = Never**
Score	**Question**
	1. Are you able to listen all the way through someone's point (even a long-winded person), allowing them to finish what they are trying to say before you speak?
	2. When someone hesitates do you encourage them to finish rather than start your reply?
	3. Do you allow the person speaking to finish his or her idea before you judge what is being said?
	4. Are you able to appraise what is being said without judgment, even when you don't like the person who is speaking?
	5. Do you give the speaker your full attention while listening – avoid looking at your phone, watch, etc.?
	6. Are you able to maintain eye contact and affirm what is being said with a nod or verbal signal?
	7. Are you able to stay focused, regardless of the speaker's grammar, accent, or word choice?
	8. Do you ask questions to clarify what is being said?
	9. Do you mirror back key points to make sure you have heard and understand what they said correctly?
	10. Can you listen even when you believe you know what is going to be said?

So...how did you do? Total Your Numbers and Rate Your Skills

Score	Indicator
35-40	**Great!** You are an attentive listener. Chances are others view you as such.
29-34	**Very Good!** A little effort would move you to the next level.
24-28	**Needs Some Work.** Identify your lowest ratings. How does your lack of skill/attention in these areas interfere with hearing others' opinions and ideas? What would be the benefit of improving?
< 23	**Danger Zone.** Take a careful look at your answers. This may be a good area of focus for your ongoing development.

Bonus Points: This is how you see yourself. But how would someone else see you? Try this evaluation again, but this time have someone who knows you well answer the questions with you in mind. Encourage feedback and listen to their comments. Remember, having a problem in any area of our lives is an opportunity to change and receive the reward!

Part 5: Question Time

Answering Various Question Types

As noted earlier, the best interviewers blend formats and question types for the greatest effect. Remember that interviews (unless stress-oriented) are not designed to be adversarial. A good recruiter or hiring manager should want to see your best. You must be prepared enough to answer all "stock" questions, yet be flexible and creative enough to respond to complex questions without sounding robotic or rehearsed. Question types include:

General Information Questions

These obtain factual information while testing your communication skills, long- and short-term planning, and ability to organize simple ideas. Examples include:

- Why do you want this job?
- What type of work do you enjoy?
- What are your strongest skills?
- What are your long-range goals, and plans for achieving them?
- Do you like to work individually or as part of a team?
- Are you willing to relocate?
- Are you willing to travel? If so, to what degree?
- Are you willing to spend six months as a trainee or contractor?

Behavioral Questions

Based on the idea that past performance is the best way to predict future behavior, these questions try to establish a pattern of performance. They are particularly useful in that they can be tailored to the specific needs of the organization. Keep in mind that an effective answer will include:

- A description of the **challenging** situation you faced
- An explanation of the process or **actions** taken
- A description of the outcome or the **results** achieved

As you can see, these line up to form the CAR statements we reviewed in Phase 2 of this book – "Building a Rock Star Resume." Use these examples to respond to both competency-oriented and job- or skill-specific questions. When speaking with your interviewer you can earn "extra points" by providing a summary of what you learned from the experience or project. This not only demonstrates a willingness to continuously improve, it also shows that you actively seek and apply feedback from others on completed projects.

Character Questions

These questions are ideal for learning about your personal attributes such as motivation and integrity. Examples include:

- How would you describe yourself?
- What rewards do you look for in a career?
- Of what accomplishments are you most proud?
- Do you work well under pressure?
- How would you handle a conflict with a colleague or manager?

Stress Questions

These are helpful in discovering how you act under pressure. They are also used to clarify issues the interviewer may see as potential problems. Examples include:

- Why do you think you are the best candidate for this job?
- Why do you want to leave your present position?
- Why have you held so many/few jobs?
- What is your weakest point?
- Have you ever been fired?
- Does your present employer know you are planning to leave?

Inappropriate/Illegal Questions

There are some questions that can damage the organization either legally or via negative word of mouth. Though often asked by inexperienced interviewers, with benign intentions, these questions can cause considerable friction between the parties and can damage your performance on the interview. Be on the lookout for the following illegal/inappropriate questions:

- How old are you?
- Are you married?
- Do you have children?
- Do you own a home?
- What is your nationality?

Reality Check

Remember, you are not obligated to answer the questions listed above. Some people believe that refusing to do so can mark you as a "difficult" candidate and reduce your chances of obtaining a position. This is not the case. You should never answer a question you feel is irrelevant or personally intrusive. Instead, try to discern whether the question is innocent or formed with ill intent. If the latter, call them on it. There is always another job. Nothing is worse than compromising your personal beliefs or integrity.

Note: The above section is written from a U.S. perspective. Other countries have different laws, procedures, practices, and cultural norms. As one of the more litigious countries, the U.S. has some of the most stringent practices in this area. If seeking a job in another country, be prepared for questions that could seem unorthodox from an American perspective.

Understanding the Answer Evaluation System

While first impressions and personal opinions are important in determining a candidate's value, both are subjective measures. To ensure candidates are examined on a level field, employers often take the time to establish customized, position-based evaluation criteria. Many employers use a weighted skill checklist to rank candidates. Others design a "wish list" job description and compare candidates to that ideal. Skilled interviewers take this a step further by determining beforehand the kind of answers they are seeking for each question. This allows them to rate candidates on each specific area, rather than going with a general reaction.

For example, given the assumption that potential employees should take the time to conduct useful research, the interviewer can look for candidates who know:

- General information about the company and industry
- Ownership of company, product/service lines, geographic spread, mission, vision, and potential growth
- Information about specific jobs and projects
- Industry buzzwords and jargon

While it is difficult to know beforehand the criteria being used, you can increase your chances of doing well through research, networking, and preparation.

Ask the Interviewer Effective Questions

An interview is a two-way street. You can and should ask the interviewer a series of well-formed questions. Typically these are asked toward the end of the meeting, but you should feel free to ask them throughout the session. Anything you can do to make the meeting feel more like a discussion between colleagues will work to your benefit.

"Good questions" depend on your level and experience. Clearly, a person seeking an intern role will have different focus areas than someone in line for a global VP position. The following are sample questions. Discuss additional options with your career coach.

- Can you describe a typical workday for someone in this position?
- How will the responsibilities of the position expand over time?
- Can you tell me about the people I'd be working with?
- Can you tell me the good and bad of the job?
- What are your expectations in the first ninety days?
- How can the successful candidate make your life easier?
- Of all the responsibilities we discussed, what would be the biggest win for this role in the first year?
- What is the career path?
- What are the conditions necessary for advancement?

Self-Guided Exercise 25: Getting to Great Questions

Remember, the type of question you ask will give an indication of your focus, interest, preparation, and competency level. Consider what the following weak questions say about the communicator. Fill in the chart below with your reactions.

Question	What It Says About the Person
• What does this company do?	• Hasn't done any research
• What does the work group look like?	•
• How much vacation time do you get?	•
• Will you pay for my continued education?	•
• What kind of office will I have?	•
• What time do I have to be at work?	•

Coach Exercise 12: Return Fire – Your Interview Questions

Role-play: Now ask your coach other well-formed questions. Why would they convince the interviewer that you would be an excellent hire?

It is important that you emulate success throughout the process. What you actually know is important, to be sure, but often your communication skills and style are the keys to advancing for further consideration and ultimate selection. Make sure you spend the time to ensure you are interview-ready.

Part 6: Making Your Mark

Making a Good First Impression

Small talk. Oh great, just what we introverts were hoping for! But as much as we'd like to *get down to business*, a big part of success in the interview process comes from an ability to initially connect and continue to develop rapport with the hiring manager and other stakeholders. Again, this book is not alleging that introverts are ill-equipped for the task – many of us are quite good at building rapport, especially in a one-to-one or small-group setting – it's just often not our first choice of activities.

When something is viewed with a chore-like mindset, e.g., "I *have to* go to that office party"; "I really *must* do more networking," it can come across in negative ways that you may not consciously perceive. To combat this natural tendency it's important to understand the communication process and how to control the verbal and nonverbal indicators you send. This begins with the first impression.

Seasoned interviewees understand that a first impression is formed by the subconscious mind within thirty seconds of meeting someone new. We base these impressions on cultural norms, personal preferences, biases, and learned expectations derived from organizational requirements.

While first impressions may not always reveal your true nature, they are an important factor in the overall assessment. For example, introverted individuals can be misinterpreted and passed over if the interviewer relies too heavily on the first impression. Luckily, there are ways to compensate for actual or perceived shortcomings. To be successful you must understand and master them all. The following factors contribute to a first impression:

Attitude

Attitude is the most influential factor in opinion formation. It encompasses several characteristics that appeal directly to our subconscious mind. When you exhibit one or more of these traits in a positive sense, the interviewer is often left with the feeling that you are highly competent (whether or not that is the case).

Understanding the power of attitude will help you make a good impression that reflects positively on the rest of the interview process. To exhibit a positive attitude, demonstrate:

- Enthusiasm – Act like you want the job

- Self-confidence – Act like you deserve the job (without being cocky)
- Vibrancy – Display a sense of passion for the profession in general
- Intelligence – Demonstrate company knowledge and an inquisitive nature
- Charisma* – Be consistently charming/pleasant even when "off" the hot seat

*As a speaker, trainer, and facilitator I've long been able to display a high level of humor and charisma during the sessions. Because of this, when I was teaching a session on personal styles, participants would be convinced that I was an off-the-chart extrovert. Of course this has a lot to do with the setting (me as speaker on stage), but many would be flabbergasted when I revealed my own MBTI scores. I (and probably you) can be flexible when the occasion calls for it, but I often need to recharge in preparation for the next training session or speaking gig.

If you find the simple thought of having to be *on* – engaging in a marathon of chitchat – exhausting, fear not. Charisma is actually something you can learn and wield like any other tool when the occasion calls for it. Olivia Fox Cabane does a masterful job of explaining this in her book *The Charisma Myth*.

Image and Appearance

Though many companies have considerably relaxed their dress policies, the interview is still a place for corporate attire. Remember, each employee is a representative of the organization. As such, hiring managers will make an assessment about how you would reflect on them and represent yourself to their clients based on how you show up. Additionally, as silly as it sounds, how you look gives clues as to whether you fit the norms of their organization. To be effective you should:

- Dress conservatively.
- Wear no excess jewelry.
- Mind your hair and shoes.
- Maintain good personal hygiene, and that includes going easy on the perfume or cologne. (My advice is to skip them entirely. Interviews are not dates.)
- Be awake, alert, and ready for a lively discussion.

Again, these may seem like "no-brainers," but they matter. You don't want to be the brown shoe guy in a black suit company. When in doubt, overdress.

Communication

The notion that 90 percent (or some rough percentage) of communication is comprised of nonverbal messages is a common assertion. People often cite general research or undocumented studies to enhance the validity of the claim. While the nonverbal portion of a message is critical, such declarations are false, and in many cases arise from a misinterpretation of the research.

It doesn't take a scientist to prove the point. Try watching the news with the sound off. Can you really capture 90 percent of the message? What about phone calls? According to this theory, they would border on useless – after all, you are missing out on the person's body language. Clearly, I'm being dramatic.

Verbal and nonverbal communication become important when the two are in conflict. For example, if I ask how you are feeling and you say "Fantastic," but your shoulders are slumped, your tone is deflated, and you can barely muster the energy to look at me, I'd be more apt to believe the nonverbal indicators. In other words, I heard what you said, but the nonverbal communicators speak the truth.

Why is this important? Well, during an interview your nonverbal communication should match, support, and enhance the actual message you convey. If you tell me you are an experienced presenter while stuttering and struggling to make eye contact, you will lose credibility whether or not the claim is accurate.

Be mindful of the signals you send. Everyone gets sick, loses sleep, gets nervous, or just has an off day. A trained interviewer will look for discrepancies in what you say and how you say it. Make sure you control the images you send so he or she can form an accurate impression. We will explore this in greater detail in the next section.

Qualifications

Logically speaking, it is impossible for an interviewer to gain any indication of your qualifications in the sixty to ninety seconds it takes to form a first impression. Still, most novice interviewers assume they can get a sense of candidate's qualifications during the introduction process. Understand, though, that any impression is merely a residual effect from having reviewed your resume. Regardless of whether it's "fair," it is natural for them to draw conclusions regarding your qualifications from this brief, subjective observation. Thus, it is critical to master your attitude, image, and communication. Once you lose points it is hard to win them back.

Read, Analyze, and Evaluate an Interviewer's Body Language

Self-Guided Exercise 26: Test a Friend – Nonverbal "OK" Exercise

Instructions: *Ask a friend or colleague to focus on you. Hold up an "OK" sign and ask them to do the same. Now ask them to place the OK on their chin while you do the same (but you quickly put yours on your cheek). Which direction do they follow – the one they saw or the one they heard? Most will follow what they saw you do, demonstrating of the power of nonverbal communication* **when in conflict** *with verbal messages.*

Lesson: *Respect the power of nonverbal communication. As you can see, it is more powerful and more believable than its verbal counterpart – when the two are in conflict.*

Coach Exercise 13: The Power of Body Posture

Instructions: *Sit in a way that would indicate a poor nonverbal communicator. (Slouch, shoulders rounded, head down, shallow breaths, frown, etc.) Really play the part. Have fun! Now quickly shift your mindset to that of a positive person who exemplifies a knowledgeable, powerful, confident communicator.*

Quick Tip: *Did you change your physicality? Most do. If so, what did you change? Discuss your observations with your coach. It's hard to disconnect your physical frame from your mental outlook. If you're nervous before an interview, you can actually trick yourself into a more confident frame of mind by assuming a better body posture.*

Understanding nonverbal communication will increase the effectiveness of your interview. Everyone comes to the interview polished. Nonverbal communication offers the interviewer cues as to what you are really like. You can't charm your way into a job that is not a good fit. There are too many telltale signs. Be honest and put the time in to understand what your nonverbal communication says about you. A powerful nonverbal communicator will:

- Appear comfortable but engaged
- Extend a firm handshake
- Maintain eye contact
- Demonstrate good posture and sit still

- Smile comfortably
- Convey warmth, trustworthiness, and sincerity
- Mirror, match, and lead the interviewer

Read, Analyze, and Evaluate an Interviewer's Verbal Cues

Of course, you can never discount the power and importance of verbal communication. This is especially critical if you seek a managerial position, or one that requires customer contact or team interaction. A powerful verbal communicator will:

- Take charge of the interview by introducing him or herself
- Use positive words when discussing his or her accomplishments
- Be respectful about prior employers and managers
- Use correct grammar, avoiding slang and language that is too informal
- Avoid credibility robbers such as "just," "little," "small," "I guess," and "probably"
- Consciously guide the conversation toward personal strengths
- Demonstrate personality by comfortably engaging in pre-interview small talk
- Demonstrate a sense of humor and humility
- Maintain pleasing voice characteristics, including tone, pacing, and pitch

Coach Exercise 14: The Power of Verbal Communication

> *Instructions: Ask your coach a sample interview question. Have him or her answer in a way that would indicate a good verbal communicator. Then have him or her answer the same question in a manner that would indicate a poor communicator. Ask for observations and differences. Now switch roles and try your hand at the productive version. How do you come across?*

Part 7: Closing the Interview

Turning the Tables ... Gently

In a recovering job market (and in any economy for in-demand roles) competition for topnotch candidates is high. To attract and retain quality employees, interviewers need to actively promote their organization and the benefits of becoming part of the team. While salary is certainly a major consideration, research shows that it is not an effective long-term motivator.

Savvy job seekers – especially coveted "early talent" or Gen Y/Z candidates – desire a more holistic Employee Value Proposition (EVP), which can include items as diverse as stock options and the company's stance on social responsibility. Employees respond increasingly to ancillary benefits and flexibility in the workplace. Make sure you understand both company benefits and the organizational style. These include:

- **Classic Benefits:** Health, dental, and life insurance, and 401k and matching
- **Ancillary Benefits:** Legal insurance, tuition reimbursement, pension plan, stock options, casual dress, and travel rewards
- **Family-Oriented Benefits:** Flex-time, job share, childcare, and telecommuting
- **Organizational Benefits:** Career development, timely reviews, job sharing, and mentoring programs

Note: This is a topic best left for the second or third interview. Also, it is advised that you wait until you have an offer before asking detailed questions about or trying to negotiate benefits.

Obtaining Feedback

Feedback is always helpful, especially when you do not get the position. If rejected, ask for a short debriefing session to help in your search. You can also ask for feedback at the close of the interview if it becomes apparent that you are not right for or do not want the position. The resulting conversation may also bring to light additional skills that may align you to another position. To take feedback correctly you should:

- Be enthusiastic and willing to learn.
- Inquire about skill gaps, missing experience, and areas of weakness.

- Ask for suggestions for improvement.
- Listen and be open to what they have to say.
- Don't debate them. Remember, you asked for their view – accept it.
- Understand that they could be wrong. Don't live and die by what they say. It is only one person's opinion.

Never Be Discouraged

My license plate says "PERSIST." I know that is incredibly cheesy and I deserve every bit of the good-natured ribbing from my friends. It used to be worse. Years ago, it said "BELIEVE." Of course, that didn't help my dating life. I'd get out of my car and some joker would inevitably say, "Good morning, Father. How are you?"

Nevertheless, I *believe* in looking at the bright side – a message that comes through in my training sessions, keynote speeches, and hopefully my everyday interactions. Of course, sometimes you are tested in your career and it's easy for a positive outlook to fade in the face of layoffs, missed opportunities, or unattained promotions.

I faced such a test when I sought to switch careers. After having a successful career in the trading industry I pursued an internal consulting role in the organization development space. I thought my business skills and experiences would transfer easily to the profession. And since I'd been an adjunct instructor at several local colleges I believed the added experience in the learning and development space would seal the deal. Feeling confident, I also assumed my "status" in the prior profession would transfer, perhaps expediting my rise in the new organization.

As you might have guessed, reality proved a little less accommodating. The hiring manager tactfully informed me that I was in no way ready for the role and suggested I build my credentials in the discipline before aiming so high. I have to admit that I was a little ticked off at first, but after I imagined him seeking a spot as a fuel trader I had to laugh at my bravado.

Rather than waste more time, I took a series of roles and contract work in smaller organizations, nonprofits, and startups. In short order I was playing at that level. Soon after, I was able to leverage skills obtained from both experiences to rise even higher in the corporate setting.

Salary Negotiation

Salary negotiation is perhaps the most challenging part of the interview process. Being prepared, however, can make things significantly easier. The following tips will help considerably:

1. Avoid giving a salary requirement or, worse, your current salary. Most employers will make you an offer on the lower end of their range. To keep the upper hand, delay discussions until they ask. Once they commit to a number, you can counter with a higher figure.

2. When asked about your current salary, softly turn the tables by inquiring as to the company's "typical range" for the position.

3. If they press the issue, provide your salary expectations in the next role. **Note**: I recommend taking the same approach with online forms. We have been brainwashed to believe that we must to give a relative stranger our personal financial details because they might be in a position to offer us a job. If an online form forces an entry for current salary, I include my *desired* salary and note at the bottom of the form or in the cover letter that "all compensation figures are reflective of current salary expectations."

4. It's rare that an interviewer will halt the process if you refuse to divulge your current compensation. However, if they press the issue and you truly feel pressure given your current circumstance to secure the role, give them the industry average adjusted up for cost of living. This will require research, but is well worth the trouble. Frankly, I'd rather not work for a company that uses this shortsighted, invasive, and largely irrelevant approach, but we all have mouths to feed, so in the end do what you are most comfortable with given your situation.

5. When they make an offer, *always* ask for an additional concession. This could come in the form of straight salary, additional vacation, or an ancillary benefit such as a sign-on bonus. Never agree to the first offer.*

* Of course, the *always* rule isn't always true. There are times when you shouldn't debate the issue. These include:

- Tight market conditions: Don't penny-pinch during a recession
- When the position offers considerable long-term career growth
- When the role is a stretch above what you currently do
- When you are competing with more experienced candidates, if known

Note: Recruiters and hiring managers typically judge their offers based on what you currently earn, a practice which is as frustrating as it is nonsensical. Like-for-like roles rarely exist. If you're looking to make more, thoughtfully build a business case before you start the negotiation process. Leverage points for moving up in salary could include:

- Moving from a nonprofit to a public company
- Moving to a more expensive area
- Comparative size of the new company
- Comparative scope of the new role
- Number of people managed
- Financial health of the organization

Also, don't leave money on the table by failing to consult the calendar. If you are due for a raise, bonus, or other perk (such as a tuition reimbursement) in three months or less, make sure that is factored into the final offer.

Coach Exercise 15: Time to Negotiate

Role-play: Practice negotiating with your coach – make it real by using relevant salary figures and working through the "what's your current salary?" question.

Closing with Confidence

Like the opening, the closing of an interview leaves a powerful impression in the mind of the interviewer. To ensure that you leave him or her with a positive view (whether or not you are still in the running) do the following:

- Invite additional questions
- Clarify the hiring-process procedures and the time frame involved
- Ask for an appropriate follow-up procedure if not immediately scheduling a second interview

- Thank the interviewer for his or her time
- Offer a firm handshake

Coach Exercise 16: Close Strong

Role-play: *Now practice closing an interview with your coach. Be sure to use terminology and job descriptions relevant to your position.*

Tips From The Trenches – Staffing And Coaching Pros Speak Out

Purpose

Although *The Introvert's Guide to Job Hunting* provides a practical, practitioner-oriented view of the job search based on both detailed research and my experience in the field, I thought it would be helpful to supplement the work with thoughts, tips, and tactics from a variety of seasoned professionals.

Description

This section offers tips from several experienced, high-performing experts in the staffing and job search process. Each person interviewed has a specific sub-specialty that will provide additional insights to the three phases noted above. Whether you are a college intern seeking your first job or a seasoned corporate leader looking to obtain your next executive role, the knowledge provided by my colleagues will help you achieve your career objectives. This section will cover:

- Assessment, resume, and interviewing tips for candidates in various stages of their careers, including:
    o Executives
    o Professional and managerial staff
    o Interns
    o Contractors
- Insights from internal corporate recruiters
- Insights from external recruiters (headhunters)
- Tips from professional career coaches
- Global insight – lessons from recruiters in Europe, Asia, and Latin America
- Special advice for introverts and extroverts

Tips from the Experts

Over the course of my career I've been fortunate enough to work with some incredibly talented professionals. These internal staffing experts, external recruiters, and career coaches offer a wealth of experience in the field.

Each person highlighted below offers a unique perspective on the job-hunting process. Their collective wisdom complements the material in this book. It will ensure that regardless of which career stage you are in – intern to executive – you will have the tools you need to secure the role you desire.

External Staffing Pros – Headhunters

Karen Russo is the owner of K. Russo Consulting, Inc. and IIPE Executive Research, two organizations that specialize in senior-level recruiting in the HR, communications, and C-suite space for a variety of industries in North and South America. She has over twenty years of experience in staffing, with a specific focus on mid- to top-tier talent.

How important is goal-setting/career self-assessment to securing the position you desire?

This is critical. The exercise can help ensure your career goals are aligned to your life goals. Job seekers should think about what they want to accomplish and then set a plan in motion to achieve it. For example, if you want to work internationally in five years, make sure your next job sets you up for that opportunity.

Job seekers should benchmark their skills and revisit their goals at least once per year. Compare your self-view with what others – including your current manager – are telling you. This exercise can provide valuable insight on skills you can leverage, qualities or experiences you might be missing, and even blind spots you never knew were there. You can then develop a plan to close the gap.

Finally, don't be afraid to check your value in the market. You might be surprised.

What are the secrets to crafting a good resume?

Like everyone these days, staffing professionals are incredibly busy. Your resume has about twenty seconds to make a positive impression. That means more than simply being formatted correctly and error free. You have to be specific, brief, and relevant to the job and, if possible, the organization. Make it difficult or miss the basics and it may get tossed into the circular file.

An important way to stand out is a meaningful professional summary. Use action-oriented keywords that showcase your best features and then back them up with examples of accomplishments and strategies that support your claims.

Since most resumes are emailed, include hyperlinks to prior companies, especially if moving to a different industry. Even external recruiters will not be familiar with every organization. Having a quick way to assess the size and scope of places you've worked and roles you've held is very helpful. Also make sure your resume and LinkedIn profile tell the same story. And while we're on the subject of LinkedIn – be professional. Pictures count. Save the casual ones for Facebook.

What are your *must do* interview tips? Are there any bad moves to avoid?
Dos

- **Style Matters** – Sometimes really sharp people forget the basics. This can be especially true for introverts, who focus less on external cues. Still, the little things are important. How you look, your dress, shoes, hair, smile, posture, fingernails, and handshake combine to create that all-important first impression. What you know matters, of course, but the medium counts just as much. You have to look the part, so dress for the role you want.

- **Do Your Homework** – Make sure you know the industry and the company's position, mission, values, and strategy. Then work to create parallels with your views and what you've done in your career. That shows knowledge while creating rapport.

- **Ask Good Questions** – Make sure you understand what they want in a candidate and what works (and doesn't work) at the company. If they have competencies for that job, great. If not, try to get a sense of what a win looks like in the role and whether or not you could deliver it.

- **Listen** – This is critical. You have to **actively** listen to the interviewer – not only for content, but for their "hidden agenda." As you move through the conversation try to uncover what they are struggling with, what they haven't seen in other candidates that they are hoping to get from you, and what success will look like in the near and long term. Specifically, try to identify what the exceptional performance or expectations in the role are during the first thirty to sixty, and first ninety days.

- **Be Positive** – Regardless of your current career situation, remain positive about the organization and prior managers. If things aren't great where you are, focus on what you learned. The world is small. No one wants to hire someone who has a tendency to trash talk.

Don'ts

- **Name Drop** – Who you know may open certain doors, but once you're in, you have to prove your value based on work completed.

- **Generalize** – Resist the temptation to be vague. Sometimes candidates (especially introverts) play down their role in projects and use "we" language. Now's the time to be specific and clearly state what you did, the process you used, and the results you achieved. Sure, you can mention others, but be clear about your role.

- **Play Defense** – We've all had career missteps and wrong turns – whether it's being laid-off or accepting a position that proves to be a bad fit. The important thing is to be up front about your career history and optimistic about what's next. You have to own your choices.

- **Be Rude** – This seems like a no-brainer, but it can show up in many ways. From leaving your mobile phone on to talking too much, or even trying to control the interview. There's a fine line between being confident and being overbearing. Don't cross it.

- **Fail to Listen to Your Headhunter's Advice** – We have a vested interest in doing right by both the hiring company and the candidate. To make the right match we do a lot of research and know the players really well. If we take the time to brief you on the hiring manager, the process, or hidden agenda, take the coaching to heart.

Generally speaking, introverts can struggle with the interview process – any tips for them?

Sometimes it's helpful to leverage your strengths. Introverts can do that by approaching the interview as if it were a project. Preparation is a key component of this and can include researching the company and the hiring manager as well as having success stories at the ready. You can also prepare by asking a trusted friend or colleague to role-play some questions. And don't forget to ask your recruiter for feedback.

Introverts, because they have a strong internal frame of reference, have a tendency to get distracted, withdraw, or visibly internalize when other people are speaking. It's not that you are not listening; it's just that you don't *look like* you're listening. Mind your body language. Try not to "go inside yourself." This can show up in a variety of ways. Slouching, for example – don't be the proverbial tall girl who doesn't want to be tall. Be proud of who you are and let it come through. You have to be willing to share more of yourself during an interview, and that includes your passion for the work and the feeling that you had when you achieved a success. So be sure to smile when you are talking about successes.

Lastly, try to connect with the person early on and maintain that connection throughout the interview. This can be accomplished through humor, stories, or simply relating to a hobby or visual cue that seems important to them.

Others may struggle with the preparation/research portion of the job search process – any words of wisdom?

Extroverts sometimes rely too heavily on their ability to build relationships through dialogue. This can result in an overconfidence that leads to a lack of preparation or an inability to stay on target and remain concise.

Because they are more comfortable in the interview setting, extroverts can also lack control and over-share. This can result in a variety of mistakes, including namedropping, being long-winded, or even non-listening. Extroverts tend to circle the question but never answer it. To overcome this they really need to focus on the other person and his/her body language.

How does the process change for internal vs. external candidates?

There is no hard and fast rule on this. In some companies, internal candidates have an edge. In other organizations it's the reverse. It really depends on the needs of the organization and how its leaders view talent. For example, some companies take pride in growing talent, others opt for a buy strategy, and some hyper-focus on diversity as a source of differentiation.

It's hard for an external person to know the rules of the game, but internal candidates should and that's where the advantage lies.

Any other free advice you'd like to offer job seekers?

Here are a couple of things to keep in mind as you look for a new position:

- Be yourself, be relevant, be engaged.
- Learn how to read your audience and adjust on the fly.
- Know your differentiator and how to work it into the conversation. Make sure you can demonstrate how you are the answer to their question.

- Don't get frazzled when interviewers don't show their cards. They might not.
- The first five minutes are the most important – you have to show something at the start. You have to start clean, crisp, and interesting.
- Make sure you come prepared with good follow-up questions. For example:
  - What are your expectations of success in the first three, six, and twelve months?
  - What is a typical day here?

How do the interview and job search processes change on the international front? Any specific differences in Latin America?

You have to be mindful of the cultural differences and how those affect the interview process. The way things are done can be surprising to a U.S. audience. Some key differences include:

- Employee contracts are the norm.
- Less discrimination issues in Latin America. For example, in Mexico you can say, "I'm looking for a male aged thirty to forty-five."
- Unions are more prevalent and influential. They have a huge impact on compensation and HR practices.

In general, be prepared to be surprised. Everything is different: labor laws, benefits offerings, even the how women and men interact in the workplace. If you are looking to move to Latin America for a role, do your homework.

Coaching Corner – Advice from Executive Coaches

Neal Nadler is founder and principal of World Associates, a consulting group focused on organization strategy and effectiveness. He is an executive and managerial coach with specific experience in Human Resource systems, practices, and strategy. He is an Organizational Training and Development professional with over thirty-five years' experience in corporate, academia and consulting. He's worked in over fifty countries, with particular expertise in the Middle East.

How important is goal-setting/career self-assessment to securing the position you desire?

Essential. Candidates that have a firm idea of who they are and what they want in a career have the best and quickest results. Some helpful assessments in making this determination are the Strong-Campbell Interest Inventory and the Holland Code Inventory. The key is to have a goal and a plan for reaching it.

Too many people abandon the job-search process as soon as they get the first bit of interest. Job searching or career management is an ongoing process. It doesn't end once you've been hired. I recommend continuing the research process even when happily employed. This doesn't mean an active overt search, but you should check the market once a year to see what you are worth and examine alternatives. People who know there are options will be less fearful and truer to who they are.

This strategy has the advantages of keeping your network fresh and allowing you to remain tuned to the needs of the market. If you stop getting recruiting calls, it may be time to research what changed and how you can refresh your skill profile to regain the momentum.

What are the secrets to crafting a good resume?

It's threefold. First, the job seeker must understand the culture of the organization and the culture of the country from which the position is being hired. In Europe, for example, a curriculum vitae works best, whereas in the U.S. a resume is the norm.

Second, you need to frame your experience in terms the recruiter and hiring manager will understand. I recently worked with two retiring generals from the U.S. armed services, and their resumes were replete with military acronyms. While these were acceptable in the *old world*, they become a detractor in the private sector. If you are changing industries, careers, or fields of expertise, you need to research the *new world* and use its verbiage to describe your past experience.

The third secret is honesty. Resumes do nothing more than get you an interview. They will help get you the best interview with the greatest chance for a fit, if they are reflective of your actual experience and align naturally with the needs of the hiring manager. In this regard, if you are not comfortable with your resume, it will show in the interview.

What are your *must do* interview tips? Are there any bad moves to avoid?

Like any endeavor, the basics are critical. To do well in an interview you have to prepare, practice, listen intently, and answer the questions asked. It's important to find natural connection points and ways to insert your key skills and achievements into the conversation, but don't blow smoke. Skillfully redirecting the conversation or changing gears is an art that takes practice. Make sure you don't force things or come off as rehearsed.

Also, take an interest in the hiring manager throughout the process. Remember, while you are convincing them, they need to convince you. In a way, you are interviewing a new boss.

Of course there are some things to avoid. These include such basics as talking too much, not answering questions, using jargon or slang, and simply under-preparing for the interview. In addition, people typically fail to understand the nonverbal cues that can give insight during an interview. These differ by region and culture, but they are worth reviewing if you know the background of the hiring manager.

Generally speaking, introverts can struggle with the interview process – any tips for them?

Yes – introverts tend to think before they talk. Do not be afraid to buy yourself time by saying, "That is an excellent and/or complex question. Give me a moment to think about it." Just recognize you can only do it once or twice per interview.

It's also a good idea to have a pad and pencil to take notes and/or write ideas down during the interview. Not only can this slow the pace of conversation, it subconsciously puts you in a like-for-like state, i.e., you are both taking notes as if it were a normal business meeting.

Finally, preparation is key. If you put in the work up front, you're more likely to make a good first impression.

Others may struggle with the preparation/research portion of the job search process – any words of wisdom?

Some aspects of the research process are more geared to introverts, but that doesn't mean extroverts are out of luck. While you still must do your due diligence in terms of reviewing the company's site and hiring manager's LinkedIn profile, much of your research can be done live via networking. The Internet is important, but it's not the only way to get things done. Extroverts can turn a hassle to an advantage by going old school with their research methods. Leverage your online social networks, but make sure you take advantage of real-world events as well.

How do things change on the international front – looking for a job outside the U.S. or working in the U.S. as an expat?

Beware of culture-based or sports-related idioms such as "Take the ball and run with it." Such sayings are common in the U.S. but you'll earn a proverbial penalty flag everywhere else. Either play it safe and steer clear of such sayings, or learn the culture of the particular region or country and adopt their sayings – if and only if you are comfortable with them and can get them right.

You also need to mind your nonverbal communication when interviewing outside the U.S. Using your left hand in the Middle East or using the "OK" sign in the Far East, for example, can cost you.

Finally, the whole process is elongated when looking outside your home country. Even if your current organization is sponsoring the job move, to contain costs most of the interviewing will be done over the phone or via video. Regardless of the process or the reasons for your move it's helpful to research the culture in advance. Joining LinkedIn groups that focus on the profession and location can provide some insight. In the end, the need for research increases when you add the complexity of culture. This is true even if you are working within your home country for a foreign-owned or -managed organization.

How does the process change for internal vs. external candidates?

External candidates are a clean slate. If the organization values new blood or perceives an internal talent gap this can be a clear plus. The trouble is, it's hard to know that from the outside. However, asking about the tenure of the management team, the hiring manager, and your potential colleagues during an interview can provide insights to the current reality.

Internal candidates are open books in many ways. Depending on the transparency rules within your organization, hiring managers could have visibility to past performance reviews, talent management scores, and succession planning data if applicable. Of course, they will also be privy to the water-cooler chat that can frame how you are actually viewed by the organization and its leadership. Internal candidates should acknowledge this reality and endeavor to work the system by building informal networks to compile support and recommendations.

Regardless of whether you are internal or external, all candidates should get in the habit of compiling success stories, lessons learned, and positive feedback to help build the case for their advancement.

Any other free advice you'd like to offer job seekers?

Sure, here are a couple of quick tips:

- **Begin Early** and expect it to take time and effort. The first job offer may take three to six months or more, depending on your industry and level. You also have to factor in the local market conditions.

- **Don't Get Frustrated** – Many job seekers give up too soon and take the first job offer out of desperation. This is not good for the hiring company or the individual.

- **Be Prepared to Rework Your Resume** – Sometimes you are qualified and should earn an interview, but your resume prevents your skills from shining through. If you consistently fail to get past the first gatekeeper consider revising your resume and/or taking a hard look at the level to which you are applying. On the other hand, if you consistently make it to the interview phase, but fail to secure any offers, you need to consider your interviewing skills or the possibility that your resume is overpromising. The key is to look for trends in feedback and adjust accordingly.

- **Don't Take It Personally** – In the end, this is a business decision based on matching company-specific needs with skills you offer. This is not a judgment on you personally. It is – or should be – about the skills you have, the value you potentially bring to the company, and the overall fit.

- **Get a Sounding Board** – Work with a coach, mentor, or trusted colleague who can keep you honest about yourself and your skills.

Sarah Levitt is an executive coach and motivational speaker who brings two decades of business experience in operations, business development, organizational growth, and entrepreneurship to her executive practice. She has coached new entrepreneurs and established executives at UNC's Kenan-Flagler Business School and has worked with clients in many industries, including technology, finance, commercial real estate, healthcare, medicine, law, human resources, and not-for-profit.

How important is goal-setting/career self-assessment to securing the position you desire? Any tips for doing it right?

I often work with senior-level professionals who come to me when they've hit a frustration point and want to increase the satisfaction in their personal and professional lives. My job is to help these action-oriented leaders slow down the process and focus on what they really want. Sometimes, if you've been stewing a while, it's easy to slip into a *grass is greener* mentality and make a move on impulse. However, being thoughtful in your approach can help you recognize what you really want and go after it.

For example, if you enjoy mentoring, but it's not currently part of your job, you might look to build that into your current responsibilities instead of completely switching careers. In many cases, the whole of your work life isn't broken. Sometimes you simply need to tweak the current situation to increase your satisfaction.

Assessments can help with the process. I sometimes use the Values in Action (VIA) instrument from the University of Pennsylvania as a complement to coaching. It ranks people's character strengths and values, and in doing so helps them see what is really important.

Part of goal setting in the career context is to understand your deal-breakers: what you must have and what you won't tolerate. Given the challenge of changing roles at a senior level, if your current organization ticks four out of five items on your list, it might be better to make small changes than a big move. On the other hand, if your career has morphed to a place where you are fundamentally out of alignment with your current goals, it might be time to switch. Coaching and self-assessment can help clarify that choice.

What are your *must do* interview tips?

- **Have a Warm-up Interview** – My clients are high-achieving people who are quick to action. Often this means they want to shoot for the ideal role right out of the gate. If you've moved up in one organization and it's been a while since you've interviewed externally, your skills may be rusty. Even senior executives can benefit from a warm-up interview, so allow some room to get back in the game.

- **Adopt a Conversational Tone** – Authenticity is key at all levels, but is particularly important for senior leaders. Practice is important, but be sure not to come off as robotic or rehearsed. Leaders are hired as much for the impact they have as what they know. You have to let the interviewer see your genuine self – your leadership style.

- **Know Your Value** – Many people can do the job. The key is to understand and be able to convey why you are the right person for the role. You must have a compelling answer to the *why me?* question.

- **Take Your Time** – This is true in most cases, but especially if you are currently employed. Sometimes people seek to leave a situation because a single, albeit important, aspect is off. However, if you move too quickly, without proper research, the new place could be worse. To avoid inheriting a new set of problems, take time to ensure the new position is the right match and offers something that is currently missing.

- **Keep Your Perspective** – Finding a new role at the senior-most level takes time, and rightly so if you are being selective. It's important to prepare yourself for the process. Often, successful senior leaders will set the bar high and become overly critical of their performance when a match is not achieved right away. Interviews at this level are less about judging your skills than finding a fit. That takes time.

Generally speaking, introverts can struggle with the interview process – any tips for them?

Many introverts do exceptionally well in interviews because they have the ability to really connect with the hiring manager in a one-on-one setting. Don't talk yourself into a bad spot because of what others think. Know yourself and your skills, and be authentic. With a little practice and preparation you can achieve the results you seek.

Any other free advice you'd like to offer job seekers?

Here are a couple of things to keep in mind as you look for a new position:

- **Start by Understanding** what you really want and why. This includes knowing the compelling reason behind your desire to make a change. Sometimes people seek a new job because another part of their lives isn't working. Focus is critical. Understand before you act.

- **Know Your Deal Breakers** – If the job is the issue, be specific about what's missing or what's changed. Do you enjoy the work, but lack growth opportunities? Are their elements missing from your current role? Are there responsibilities that you would like to shed? Have your priorities changed and you need to reevaluate what's important? The details matter.

- **Create a Roadmap** – Take time to list and rank your must haves and deal breakers. Once you know what you want and why, you can set out to find it.

- **Consult Your Family** – You have to look at your whole life and how your decisions will affect your other interests and responsibilities. Often changes at the senior level require a move and major shift (at least initially) in workload. Make sure the family is on board before moving too far. A discussion early on will help increase understanding and support.

A European Perspective

***Nora Schoenthal** is a consultant with Development Dimensions International (DDI), and has more than a decade of experience in assessments, coaching, and people leadership, including hiring. She has worked with mid- to executive-level leaders and professionals across a variety of industries and geographies. Nora has lived and worked in the U.S. and Germany and has worked with multinational companies such as Merck, Parker Hannifin, Halliburton, Quintiles, VF Corporation, and Walmart as a consultant and executive coach. Beyond the work with clients, her experience with DDI includes the design and global rollout of executive assessment and talent management tools and solutions, as well as operational management and quality assurance of executive assessment and interview delivery.*

How important is goal-setting/career self-assessment to securing the position you desire? Any tips for doing it right?

Assessing fit is critical. If, as a hiring manager, I get the sense that you simply want a job you will be looked over. You have to want *this particular job* for a specific reason. Knowing yourself and what you want in a career makes it easier to demonstrate that you have thought through the process and can be specific about why the role is a fit for both you and the hiring organization.

There are a variety of inexpensive assessments that can help you better understand your personality and what might fit. Collecting feedback is also helpful. Just make sure the feedback is obtained from people who know you really well and will tell the truth about how you come across.

This is particularly important for introverts, who can sometimes struggle to make a good first impression. Having a mentor who helps you tap into those things that make you shine can make the process easier. With practice, talking about your achievements will seem more natural.

What are the secrets to crafting a good resume?

Don't oversell yourself. It's important to draw attention to your best work and what is most relevant to the hiring manager, but brevity and accuracy should be your watchwords. Don't be dramatic with your language. Stick to the facts. Tell me what you've done and then allow me to interpret the importance. In short, let your accomplishments speak for themselves. This is particularly important in Germany, where anything perceived as bragging or obvious exaggeration will not go over well.

Another area that speaks to relevancy and brevity concerns the amount of material contained in the resume. You don't need to detail every aspect of a thirty-year career.

Focus on your recent work and then line-item the jobs you had straight out of university. This holds true for cover letters as well. For me, they can be a waste of time if they're just fluff. If they don't have substance, skip them.

Also, I like to see a brief section on your interests, hobbies, and volunteer work. This shows the hiring manager that you are well rounded and provides a good conversation starter.

What are your *must do* interview tips? Are there any conversation killers/bad moves that people should avoid?

Dos

- **Ask Questions** – This not only provides insight into how you think and what you'd be like to work with, it also conveys your level of interest in the job and potential fit with the company. If you don't ask questions now, you won't later, and that's a red flag. So ask while you have the chance and make your questions count.

- **Answer the Questions Asked** – These days a lot of candidates are trained on behavioral interviewing techniques and/or are coached by someone before the interview. Preparation is important, but don't use my question to position your prepared answers.

- **Know Your Value** – When you get the dreaded "Why should I hire you?" question, have a clear value proposition that supplies a compelling answer. Make sure your statement highlights why the decision to hire you would be a win for you, the manager, and the organization.

Don'ts

- **Spin Me** – Don't tell me what you think I want to hear or try to steer every question back to your talking points. Give me real answers and let me evaluate the real you against the criteria for the position.

- **Brag** – There's a fine line between highlighting and bragging. Steer clear of jargon, clichés, and exaggerated language. Have examples of real work that proves your value rather than telling me that you are flexible, a team player, etc.

- **Dodge the Tough Stuff** – If you have what could be perceived as a negative – resume gaps, job-hopping, etc. – don't make me guess at the reason behind the issue. My guess might be worse than the truth. Share your backstory, the reasons for your decisions, and what you learned along the way.

Generally speaking, introverts can struggle with the interview process – any tips for them?

I'm a big fan of professional openness throughout the process. People do more damage trying to cover up potential flaws or what they perceive to be negatives. You have to know yourself and own all that comes with that person.

In general, I'll take smart over extroverted anytime. Candidates need to know their strengths and leverage them. You don't have to be bubbly to be passionate about your profession. When you are sharp, thoughtful, and make smart decisions, that shows and is valuable.

I will say that there are certain roles – sales or senior leadership positions, for example – that may be more geared to extroverts. But that doesn't mean introverts can't be customer-facing or hold the corner office. You just need to demonstrate that you have self-awareness and can manage the impact; that your natural inclination doesn't get in the way of the demands of the position. Having a clear example of how you can flex styles and then leverage other strengths to get results is critical to making your case.

Others may struggle with the preparation/research portion of the job search process – any words of wisdom?

Extroverts need to do all the same things introverts do in the job search process; they just need to leverage and control different strengths. While making conversation may come naturally, they need to avoid over-talking, over-sharing, and under-preparing, all while working hard to stay on track and actually answering the questions asked.

If extroversion leads to confidence that can be good, but you have to have substance. A good interviewer will see through the fluff. Again, knowing yourself is critical. If you get overly talkative when nervous, remind yourself to rein it in and listen more. It's all about balance.

How does the process change for internal vs. external candidates?

In general, internal candidates have the edge because they have more information about the company, the decision makers, and the role. Also, internals are known commodities, which is typically less of a risk.

That said, being known is not always a good thing if it means that leaders are locked into seeing you in a certain way and at a certain level. Sometimes people need to jump ship to advance. This gives people a chance to reinvent themselves and be viewed by impartial eyes. Often it comes down to what the organization and the hiring manager specifically value in a role.

Any other free advice you'd like to offer job seekers?

Sure, here are a few quick tips that come to mind:

- **Don't talk yourself into a job** because you think you should want it or it seems like the logical next step up the ladder. Have a well-thought-out rationale for making the move.

- **Don't act out of desperation** – Of course, this is easier said than done if you're out of work or underemployed in a tight job market.

- **Be honest about what you want** and how it fits with the rest of your life. For example, taking a job for which you are overqualified is okay if you are downshifting your career. However, if it's a force fit or emergency fix, you will feel it fast.

- **Try to get a realistic preview of the job** and corporate culture before signing on. Don't make assumptions.

- **Be thoughtful when applying**. It's tempting to mass-produce submissions with the number of tools available, but stay away from the copy-and-paste application. The flip side of this is to be careful when a company has a sloppy hiring process, or lacks one altogether. Even though no one likes to go through many steps and it is stressful, it is a way to get to know the company and for the company to make a good decision. If they hire you after one interview, it poses a risk for both sides.

Early Talent

Ali Ghiassi is a sales and recruiting professional with over seven years of demonstrated success in talent acquisition and project management in life sciences, manufacturing, engineering, and finance sectors in the U.S. and Mexico. Ali has held various leadership roles with Aerotek, Inc., and is currently tasked with driving business and managing regional delivery for their life sciences offering.

How important is goal-setting/career self-assessment to securing the position you desire? Any tips on doing it right?

Knowing what you want before you begin is a top priority. Too many people, especially those early in their careers, will take the first job that comes along. Others take a job simply because it seems like the next step. Before you make a move, you have to know what you are chasing and ensure that it will be the right step personally and professionally. For example, is it the work that attracts you to a role or are you simply seeking a new title, more money, a chance to lead, or something else entirely?

You have to be clear at the beginning.

There are a variety of assessments in the market that can help you gain clarity on everything from your personality style to what career might fit you. These include Myers-Briggs, Strengths Finder, DISC, Insights Discovery Test, Page Work Behavior Inventory (PBWI), Career Liftoff Interest Inventory, and SkillScan Assessment.

Of course, not everything can be learned from an assessment. People – the *right* people – are the key to finding and staying on the path to career success. To have the best chance of success you need to surround yourself with those who can help you get where you want to be.

Having a formal mentor is important, but be sure not to look too far ahead of the career curve. While it's helpful to have a long-term vision of where you want to be, e.g., become a rock star millionaire guru, he or she might not be the ideal mentor at your current career stage. Working with someone a few steps ahead of where you are may be more practical and produce better results.

And don't assume that someone always needs to be higher on the corporate ladder to be a mentor. You can learn a lot from peers, and even from those earlier in their careers than you are. Remember, it's not about title. It's about skill. Find someone who has a skill you need to develop and work with them. You might even be able to return the favor. Just make sure that whoever you choose to work with will give you honest feedback. Mentors should never sugarcoat things.

What are the secrets to crafting a good resume?

What you did is important, but the real value comes from the impact you had. When you effectively showcase the ROI for your efforts you can set yourself apart from other candidates. There are a variety of techniques for doing this, but at a minimum you should explain the situation you faced, the action you took, and the results you achieved. Include the most relevant and impressive of these stories on your resume and keep others in your back pocket to use as discussion points during the interview.

It's also important to keep your resume relatively brief. This doesn't mean shortchanging your work history. Just don't be redundant. If you're new to the professional workforce, there's no need to detail the nine jobs you had waiting tables throughout high school and college. Demonstrate your work history so employers know you have staying power and can balance the multiple demands of work and school, and then focus on what you learned from the experience. The same rule applies to more experienced workers. If you have twenty years of sales experience there's no need to list the ice cream stand you had as a kid. Be relevant and ensure your experience matches the job you're applying for.

As far as tactical pet peeves: Don't do anything that detracts from the professional substance of your resume. This includes using colored paper, adding a picture, or using complex formatting elements such as boxes and tables – most applicant tracking systems will jumble the data and you'll be forced to reenter any unreadable portions. As for the "resume gimmicks," remember that, even if you're in an artistic space such as web design or marketing, you should let your portfolio showcase your work. Your resume should be all business.

What are your *must do* interview tips? Are there any bad moves to avoid?
Do

- **Smile** – It's the most important (but often unrated) thing. A smile demonstrates excitement for the job and lets the interviewer know you are happy to be there. It also puts people at ease. Remember, likability is important. If hired, you'll be spending a lot of time together and people want to like those they're around. And don't forget to smile in phone interviews. It makes a difference.

- **Be Prepared** – You have to know the basics of the company and its culture, as well as who you are meeting with and, if possible, something about that person's background. You also have to know your goal and keep that in mind as the interview progresses to see if the role is truly a fit for you.

- **Practice** – Few people like role-playing, but it makes a difference. Practice the tough questions – like why you're the right person for the role. Have clear examples of success and be able to talk about mistakes and what you learned. Some people worry that they will forget everything beforehand. The goal isn't to memorize your responses. Nothing's worse than sounding rehearsed. Just bring your resume and use it as a prompt to help you recall examples.

Don't

- **Exaggerate** – Your title, your job scope, or the nature of your accomplishments.

- **Be Negative** – About former employers, managers, or anything, really. Keep it positive.

- **Be a Know-It-All** – You have to be comfortable with saying "I don't know" or "That was out of my scope" if you truly didn't own or weren't involved in a specific part of the process. Don't fake things. It's easy for someone who knows something to tell when someone doesn't.

- **Avoid Your Weaknesses** – Everyone has something they are working on. Don't act like you're Superman or Superwoman. Demonstrating an awareness of and desire to improve your development areas is a big plus. It shows that you are teachable, have a level of humility, and are willing to work.

Generally speaking, introverts can struggle with the interview process – any tips for them?

Don't create a problem. Sometimes people, introverts especially, can approach the interview as if the person on the other side of the desk is the enemy. The hiring manager isn't trying to trip you up. If anything, they are rooting for you to do well.

When a manager has an opening there is great pressure to fill it. Leverage that by showing him or her how you can fulfill their need. Also, recognize that if you got to the interview stage it's because they vetted your credentials and have decided that you belong in the candidate pool. Remember, many applicants were screened out at the resume or phone-interview stage. You're there because they want to hear from you. Now it's time to speak up.

When answering questions, take time to explain what you did and the result that action produced. Sometimes introverts get lost in their own heads. Check to make sure your audience is following along. Also, watch your body language throughout the conversation. You don't have to be over the top, but make sure you approach the process excited to learn about the person and the company, and to share your story.

What about extroverts. Any tips for them?

Extroverts will often be reluctant to admit they don't know something. To avoid this, practice your response to the "What went wrong?" question. Talking someone through a mistake, including how you corrected it and what you learned, can go a long way toward demonstrating humility and the ability to handle adversity.

Of course, extroverts should also avoid the tendency to over-share and over-talk. Dial down the bragging, name-dropping, and me/I language. There's nothing wrong with the latter, and you certainly need to be specific about what *you* achieved, but remember to note collaboration and how others helped you as well.

Any other free advice you'd like to offer job seekers?

Start by knowing what you want both in your next job and, ultimately, in your career. You have to think beyond the job description, e.g., Who do you want to impact? What type of corporate culture and size would you like? What do you want to accomplish?

Be sure to confirm your initial view of the role by interviewing people who already have the job you desire. Their answers can help you reevaluate your decisions and refocus your energy.

Finally, and this may seem counterintuitive, don't cast a wide job-search net, hoping to land anything at all. You have to research, target, and apply for roles (and companies) that match your goals and qualifications. You catch the big fish with a single line and the proper tackle. Wide nets catch bait.

- **Entry Level** – If you are new to the workforce, you'll need to focus on building a network. You also need to clarify your career intentions. A business degree, for example, seems specific, but there are many different directions you could go with that major. And remember, all your degree tells me is that you can learn, so be willing to do so when you get into an organization, as that's the expectation.

- **Blue Collar** – The reality of blue-collar jobs in the U.S. is harsh. While it may be tempting to take a job just to have something, you should take a wider view. This means being flexible and mobile. You may have to take a risk and move to take a job. White-collar workers are more accustomed to this reality, but it becoming more common for all jobs. You also have to keep learning and updating your skills to stay in tune with employer demands. Make sure you take advantage of training when offered, and complete it on your own if it's not available through your employer. It could be the element that makes the difference in the next hiring process.

Insights from Asia

Ann Léong is founder and principal of ALHRD Pte Ltd, Singapore, a consulting firm focused on creating strategic, innovative, and aligned organizations. She specializes in designing frameworks and solutions for leadership development as well as organizational-development interventions using multiple methodologies and tools. She has over twenty years of experience working with organizations, and is also a certified executive and business coach.

How important is goal-setting/career self-assessment to securing the position you desire?

We use a range of assessments and will typically work with what the client already has in place rather than introducing a new set of instruments. The most important thing is that our clients truly understand the assessments and how they complement the other elements in the hiring process.

What are the secrets to crafting a good resume?

The key is to keep your resume outcome-oriented and accomplishment-focused. Anyone can simply provide a listing of previous jobs and responsibilities. To stand out you must be able to clearly demonstrate how you can and have delivered results.

What are your *must do* interview tips? Are there any bad moves to avoid?

Top *must do*s include the following: be relevant; focus on what you did (the specific process steps) to achieve results; provide information on strategic considerations when describing previous work; be authentic; and try to maintain a conversational tone as you navigate the interview.

The following are generally considered to be bad moves: evading questions and hoping the interviewer/s won't notice; sounding rehearsed; giving only general answers even when pushed for specifics; only talking about your positive traits; and/or using throwaway examples for the "What is your biggest weakness?" questions – for example, "I work too hard." You have to be authentic.

Introverts sometimes struggle with the interview process – any tips for them?

Don't be afraid to show the interviewer your real self. It's okay if people see you as quiet or soft-spoken, or even modest. Know the inhibitions you have as an introvert and take time to develop those aspects that you are unhappy with or that could potentially hold you back from securing the desired role. For example, if your inhibitions cause people to see you as unresponsive, hesitant, or rigid, you may need to adjust how you come across. You don't want the hiring manager to mistake introversion (how you process the world around you) for a negative trait or skill gap.

Others may struggle with the preparation/research portion of the job search process – any words of wisdom?

Speak with people who work in the same industry, including some who are several years older and younger than you. Having that perspective will provide a reference point for your experience level and how you match the skill set requested in the job description. You can also use these conversations to help prepare for what may be asked in an interview.

It's also a good idea to center yourself right before the interview so that you minimize nervousness. In the end, knowing your ability to contribute to the organization should enhance your confidence, regardless of whether you are an extrovert or an introvert.

How do things change on the international front? Any specific differences within Asia?

Knowing the culture of the organization is always important. However, when you switch to an international context it's important that you develop an understanding of the local culture as well. This includes how it differs from both your home-country culture and the corporate culture. To be successful you will have to navigate all three.

In Asia, betas fare better than alphas. Alpha personalities typically express overtly dominate behavior, which can lead to a voice tone that is too aggressive and too loud, and that comes across as lecturing interviewers rather than dialoging with them. Beta personalities, on the other hand, are more likely to come across as credible, with a measured presence that doesn't claim to be better than the other person. People with this style can give the impression that he or she can collaborate effectively with different kinds of people. This doesn't make you a follower. It just means that you lead with finesse not brawn.

In the end you have to adapt to and meet the needs of the individual. Prepare, but don't make assumptions.

About the Author

Tim Toterhi is an executive coach, speaker, and leadership development professional. He is the author of over thirty articles on business best practices and coauthor of *Strategic Planning Unleashed*. He is also the founder of **Plotline Leadership**, an organization dedicated to helping people craft their success stories.

Tim has over fifteen years of experience in human resources and has held a series of global roles in organization development, talent management, leadership development, change management, and staffing operations. He has lived and worked extensively in both Europe and Asia and has experience in corporate, non-profit, academic, and consulting environments. For more information, log on to www.plotlineleadership.com.

Tim currently lives with his wife, Melissa in North Carolina. When not working, he enjoys writing fiction. He is currently working on his fifth novel. To learn more, visit www.timtoterhi.com.

About Plotline Leadership

Every story has a natural flow; a plotline filled with challenges, opportunities, and key decision points that can mark the difference between tragedy and triumph.

Individuals have their own plotlines. Whether it involves completing a project, guiding a new team, or navigating a career transition, we each have the power to draft our future.

Organizations also have a tale to tell, from setting strategy and navigating change to winning the war for talent and besting the competition. Business results often depend on our ability to set the scene and direct the players toward a clear goal.

Projects fail and careers derail when people *lose the plot* on the original intent – when they get distracted by drama, led astray by protagonists, or caught up in backstory that is simply irrelevant.

Plotline Leadership offers coaching, keynotes, and consulting services that ensure your story is a heroic adventure rather than a comedy of errors. To learn more, contact me at timtoterhi@plotlineleadership.com or via www.plotlineleadership.com.

Fiction by Tim Toterhi

Both Sides of Broken

It's hard to stop a hitman from killing your father. It's even harder when you're dead. Jonathan Holiday and his two brothers are desperate for money. Their comatose father has it, but his hospital meter is ticking away. In an effort to save themselves, the three arrange to have the abusive old man murdered. After hiring the killer, Jonathan has a change of heart. Unfortunately, he also has a suspicious accident.

Now he must battle back from a series of "After-Earths" to convince his self-absorbed, cash-strapped brothers to stop a supernatural hit man from doing his job. Both Sides of Broken is a story about defeating demons – those of this life, those in the next, and most importantly, those within ourselves.

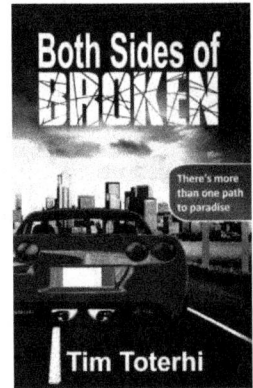

Lunches With Larry

God and a nuclear fuel broker meet in a sports bar to discuss women, work, and other life mysteries… What sounds like the start of a classic political joke, is actually the beginning of a thought-provoking philosophical adventure. Set against the scandalous decline of the largest, privately-held business empire in the nuclear brokerage industry, Lunches With Larry follows a young, romantically-challenged, business misfit on his crusade to find true love, lasting friendship, and the answer to the oldest of questions.

If you've ever felt confused, lost or all alone in a world you can't quite figure out; if you've ever thrown up your hands in frustration and shouted, "I just don't understand anything anymore," pull up chair, settle in with a spot of tea, and have a look. You may find something you've never lost and loose something you've never needed.

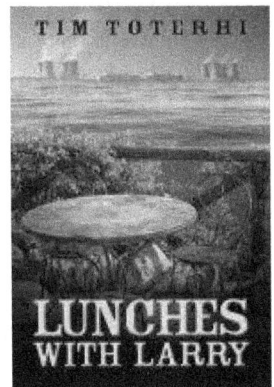

Two Minutes Too Late

We've all been there – missed the boat, missed the point, missed the chance at that something or someone special now long gone. We ache for a do over knowing full well if the wish were granted it would forever change the person we've become. Two Minutes Two Late is a collection of stories detailing the missteps of a hapless romantic. From career blunders and criminal exploits to dating debacles to goodbyes unsaid, it reminds us that while follies happen the future is unwritten and ours to explore.

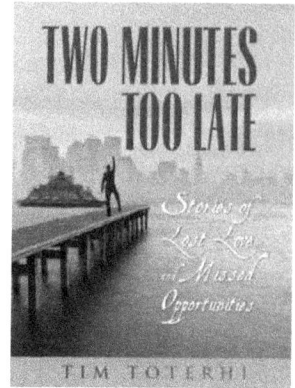

The Amazing and Somewhat Sarcastic Tad

This is a largely ridiculous coming of age adventure book set in the 1980's. It's sure to make you chuckle and aggravate any idly standing authority figures. That said it's pretty whacky so I apologize in advance for any counseling you may require after reading this work.

So here's the gist: Six Florida-based buddies struggle to maintain their youthful idealism as they travel to New York to stop a local mob boss from blackmailing their friend. During their quest they are guided by a talking tree; a partially invisible spirit-like substance; a hyper-galactic, Bee-ben-bobble playing number stealer; the evil corporate Zukes, and a semi-superhero called Barley Man. After navigating a series of moral dilemmas they stand ready to fight for life, love, and a big bucket of cash.

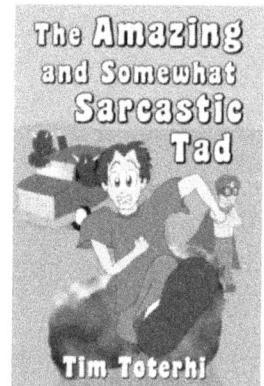

A special note for "old" people:

Sometimes parents forget to take their children seriously. Whether it be their emotional stability, their ideas on spirituality, or even something as simple as their tastes in music; somehow, some way, many kids get the feeling that you're just shrugging them off. Sad really. Perhaps we should enhance the dialogue. After all, kids have so much to say, and so much to ask.

So chill out already. Sure the book contains some off-color humor and a few whacky philosophies, but hey look on the bright side, your kid is literate. Way to go parent people! Besides, how badly can it warp their brains? I think the Internet has that covered. Loosen the reigns. Let them dream a little. Who knows, you might decide to join them.

Nonfiction by Tim Toterhi

Defend Yourself: Developing a Personal Safety Strategy

Note: Fifty percent of the author's profits resulting from the sale of Defend Yourself will be donated to RAINN. (www.rainn.org)

While most books in this category limit themselves to citing statistical data, describing case histories, or displaying various self-defense techniques, Defend Yourself! covers the entire issue in a clear, concise, workbook format. Instead of simply skimming chapters, the reader is encouraged to actively participate in the exercises within each lesson.

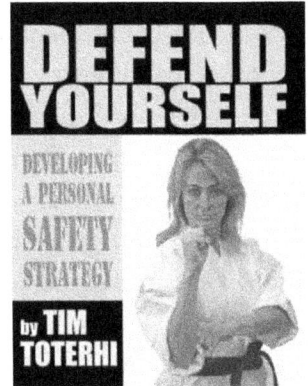

The book describes the most up-to-date prevention, empowerment, communication, and self-defense methods. In addition, the physical techniques are complemented by an in-depth analysis of potential attackers including a description of each offender type and the various modus operandi employed.

Each lesson concludes with a summary of the main points and a series of questions and exercises that will assist the reader in developing a Personal Safety Strategy. In addition, the Afterward contains a follow-up plan to help the reader keep her skills current. This is critical because a safety strategy is only useful if it is consistently used and continuously improved.

Stay safe and if you are in an abusive relationship, seek help. It's out there. You're stronger than you think!

Strategic Planning Unleashed

Despite its importance, few companies have cracked the code on strategic planning. Meetings occur, white boards are filled, and then somehow, magic happens – a binder appears, supposedly summarizing the decisions agreed to by the leadership team. Unfortunately, that is where the magic ends. The strategic plan is rarely used and left to languish on a credenza till next year.

Most strategic planning books focus on theoretical frameworks or rely on an approach endorsed by a single "ideal company". Generic models and classroom-inspired case studies rarely hold up to the rigors of the real world. And though it's true that some companies have obtained success in strategic planning, there is no guarantee that their approach will work for your organization – there is no sliver bullet!

Written by seasoned practitioners who have applied the tools in over 200 client companies, Strategic Planning Unleashed provides a practical, comprehensive playbook for each phase of the process; Environmental Assessment, Internal Capabilities Assessment, Strategy Development, and Strategy Deployment.

The methodology is scalable to different sized organizations and includes many strategic planning tools that are not in the public domain. Regardless of your company's size, complexity, offering portfolio, or geographic scope, Strategic Planning Unleashed will help your organization analyze its external environment, reach consensus on your sources of competitive advantage, identify a business strategy, and execute it seamlessly.

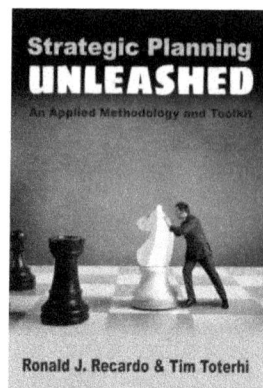

Acknowledgements

Thank you doesn't seem sufficient for the all the help, guidance, and encouragement I received during this project. Countless mentors, colleagues, and friends had a role in supporting this effort.

I am especially grateful to those who gave so freely of their time and knowledge in support of the interview section of this book. Karen Russo, Neal Nadler, Sarah Levitt, Nora Schoenthal, Ali Ghiassi, and Ann Léong – your inputs were incredibly valuable and helped advance my thinking considerably both within and beyond these pages.

Keith Miller, editor extraordinaire, many thanks for your expertise and eagle eye. You are as much a teacher as you are an editor and for that I am grateful.

The credit for internal layout and cover design goes to Stephannie Beman. Thank you for both your creativity and style. You have a rare flare for both detail and concept creation.

Finally, to my wife, Melissa, an extrovert living with an introvert – thanks for your support and understanding. I'm so glad I found you.